Performance Management

Andrew E. Schwartz
President, A. E. Schwartz
and Associates

Illustrated by Deborah Zemke

BARRON'S

All inquiries should be addressed to:
Barron's Educational Series, Inc.
250 Wireless Boulevard
Hauppauge, New York 11788
http://www.barronseduc.com

Library of Congress Catalog Card Number 99-28520

International Standard Book No. 0-7641-0883-2

Library of Congress Cataloging-in-Publication Data
Schwartz, Andrew E.
    Performance management / by Andrew E. Schwartz.
        p.   cm.
    Includes bibliographical references and index.
    ISBN 0-7641-0883-2
    1. Performance technology—Management. 2. Performance motivation.
    3. Employees—Rating of. 4. Organizational effectiveness.
    I. Title.
    HF5549.5.P37S38   1999
    658.3'1—DC21   99-28520
                                                                CIP

PRINTED IN HONG KONG
9 8 7 6 5 4 3 2

Contents

◆

DEDICATION

To all managers: Congratulations! You work toward the achievement of one of the greatest accomplishments in the world—encouraging people to be more and facilitating that growth.

ACKNOWLEDGMENTS

Special thanks to the following for their developmental input and support on this book: Melanie O'Donnell, Developmental Editor; Dawn Packer, Editor; Kate Steinbuhler, Editor; Ida Faber, Lenore Tracey, HR/OD Being, Control Technology; Dennis Zia, HR Consultant, Focus Associates; Denise Lockaby, HR Specialist, Stride Rite Corporation; Jackie Brough, HR Director, Cadec; Joan Martin, Chief of Administration & Employee Services, MBTA; Chris Bond, Manager of Training & ADA, MBTA, and SBANE.
Extended thanks to Amy Iliescu, Joel Roberts, Ben Crossman, Alison Creehan, and the FX team. Thank you to our firm's summer interns: Gregory Friedman, Michael Gottfried, Jetesh Hariramani, Carrie Holmes, Jennifer Jefferson, Elizabeth Keohane, and Elizabeth Plunkett.
As always, thanks to our firm's clients and other industry professionals.
Finally, thank you to my family.

Preface

◆

Writing on a topic of this importance in a short format was challenging. I have attempted to balance the business, academic, and practical worlds to enlighten and inform readers. The greatest gifts an author may give are the tools for readers to build skills for themselves.

In the increasingly competitive and complex business world, a company's profit margin is often determined by how effectively it utilizes and evaluates its employees. It could even be said that the very survival of these organizations depends on management's ability to make optimal use of a fair, reasonably accurate, and objective performance evaluation system. Manuals and guides for performance evaluation abound. However, I believe most lack an integrated system that encompasses not only performance appraisals, but daily performance management as well.

This book goes beyond a simple discussion of the performance evaluation and instead lays out the guidelines for effective management and how to encourage optimal performance on an ongoing basis. Managers can use this book as a valuable tool to evaluate employees and to help their employees become more effective and more productive.

A.E.S.
October 1999

Introduction

Every manager knows that employee productivity directly affects company productivity; one of a manager's primary responsibilities is to assure that each employee works as effectively and efficiently as possible. Unfortunately, many managers do not realize the pivotal role that a comprehensive performance management system can play in improving employee productivity. This enhanced productivity in turn leads to greater company-wide productivity and profit.

What is performance management? It is a style of management with its foundation in open communication between manager and employee that involves setting goals, providing ongoing feedback both from the manager to the employee and from the employee to the manager, as well as the performance appraisal. An effective performance management system helps both managers and employees to work smarter instead of harder to achieve productivity and profitability. This book describes performance management, shows how effective performance management can lead to increased profits, and outlines the manager's role in the process, including employee development, setting standards, ongoing monitoring, and aligning performance management with company goals.

This book gives managers quick and easy access to the information they need each step of the way along the path to implementing and maintaining a successful performance management system.

Once you've read this book, you'll understand the purpose and benefits of performance management systems, the components of these systems and the roles of the manager, employee, and company. You will also have concrete evidence of the success of such systems in actual businesses.

How to Use This Book

◆

This book is divided into six chapters. The first chapter introduces performance management and provides general information about companies using performance management. It also explains how to be successful and avoid pitfalls; the various roles of employees, managers, and the company; and other general information about the communication and nurturing techniques that will help make a performance management system successful.

Chapters 2, 3, and 4 dig deeper into the three main components of performance management:

◆ the manager's awareness of job description and job duties, and setting standards and understanding expectations;

◆ ongoing job performance monitoring and 360-degree feedback (two-way job performance feedback from everyone involved—customers, employees, peers, and managers); and

◆ performance appraisal.

Chapter 5 explores various options for training and development as well as compensation programs that may complement performance appraisals.

Chapter 1

Understanding
Performance
Management

One of the best things you can do for other people is help them recognize how they can improve.

—Wess Roberts

Good people make businesses successful. If you know this, then you are on your way to understanding performance management. A properly implemented and maintained performance management system does more than just retain employees—it keeps people motivated and productive. The system works because it is a continuous collaboration of employees and managers observing, giving feedback, setting and evaluating goals, planning, and coaching.

Performance management shouldn't be confused with the performance appraisal or evaluation. There are three main components to performance management:

1. understanding and setting goals and expectations

2. providing ongoing feedback

3. appraising the performance

Performance management goes beyond the quick six-month reviews that are too often used as checkpoints for an organization. An effective system should be part of the culture of an organization and needs to be present throughout a person's employment, not just at periodic intervals.

The key to performance management is in understanding the ongoing communication and planning that need to occur between employee and manager. When a company adopts a performance management model, it moves from the puppetmaster model of controlling everyone's strings toward a coaching and guidance model. Managers understand the corporate mission or goals and then guide their employees' development and performance based on these goals. When employee goals are tied to company goals, each employee feels like an important part of a team working toward a shared objective. This benefits all those involved.

To further understand performance management, think about the way your company works today. Does your company have a system for performance management? If not, is it because of lack of awareness or lack of interest? How does your company view and review its employees? Are employees threatened by reviews or do they feel that reviews are constructive? Have you ever been reviewed? In many companies, managers fall through the cracks and do not get formal reviews, much less regular feedback.

Companies are turning toward performance management systems because they work directly on motivating employees. It is becoming apparent that companies are only as good as their employees. Employees who have the support and guidance they need are more motivated and more productive, better with customers, and more likely to add to the company's worth and profitability.

Dictatorship from upper management becomes a team structure. Organizations moving from a traditional top-down type of management must realign to put responsibility and decision making ability into the hands of those doing the work. This kind of reorganization means everyone from the top to the bottom must be flexible and willing to take the ups and downs that come with major changes. It requires constant evaluation, reevaluation, and courage to change the whole system again if need be.

When employees and managers become part of a team, they often must go beyond the job description and work toward team and company goals. Job descriptions should be rough guidelines and the employee and manager should be willing to discuss and expand them as new situations arise. This tendency toward shifting goals requires the manager to ensure constant and clear communication, or employees will become frustrated.

Training and developing an employee's career skills is a vital part of performance management. People are resources, and training increases the worth of that resource for the company and the employee. To excel in a performance management system, employees should be able to learn and grow as the job evolves, and training is an integral part of this growth.

THE PURPOSE OF A SUCCESSFUL PERFORMANCE MANAGEMENT SYSTEM

◆ The system informs employees of areas in which they excel (or of their positive attributes) and of areas in which they can improve.

◆ It helps employees improve performance, increase productivity, and experience personal satisfaction and gratification.

◆ It provides the organization with information for human resource planning.

WHY PERFORMANCE MANAGEMENT?

In the age of information and knowledge sharing, managers are bombarded with techniques, tips, and systems that promise everything from easier jobs to complete health and happiness. How is performance management any different? It cuts through bureaucracy, politics, and even the minutiae of financial figures to the bottom line—the people. If employees know what is expected of them, realize that they have control over their own success, and understand their stake in the success of the company, they will be motivated and will help to boost productivity and profit.

PERFORMANCE MANAGEMENT MOTIVATES

Motivation is a basic element contributing to all types of employee performance issues. How often have you explained problem employees by saying, "They're just not motivated"?

Although this is a simple and seemingly plausible reason for poor performance, it is not entirely accurate. Everyone is motivated; however, each person is motivated by different factors and by different things. Just because your employees may not be motivated to do what you want them to do does not mean that they are not motivated.

The first step is to figure out what will motivate your employees to do what you hired them to do.

STEP ONE: GET TO KNOW THE EMPLOYEE

Begin by considering what you know about each employee. You might even want to put a motivation question on your employee self-assessment sheet. Although most people believe they deserve a better salary than they presently earn, money is not the only motivational factor. Praise, interaction with others, a desire for achievement, advancement, personal growth, and opportunities to learn are all items that motivate people. As a manager, you have the ability to offer your employees access to the things that truly motivate them.

Many problems result from the fact that an employee is more motivated not to do a task than to do it. Employees who crave attention may be quick to notice that they receive more attention when they do not finish their duties than when they complete their tasks. Employees who are expected to assist others in the department after finishing their own work are unlikely to hurry to complete their work.

STEP TWO: UNDERSTAND UNIVERSAL MOTIVATIONS

How can you use employee motivation to the best advantage? First of all, remember what motivates people. Achievement and recognition are two nearly universal factors, even though they may be manifested in different forms. Ability also contributes to motivation. Equipment and the work environment can lead to motivation or non-motivation. Ownership, or the ability to achieve without help from an outside party and the feeling of control over the company's and one's own performance, is a huge motivational factor, because this communicates to the employee that he or she is respected and trusted. Even those who enjoy working with others, like teachers or social workers, need to know that their managers trust them to do their job without constant supervision.

Achievement and Recognition

A runner who is ahead of the pack, breaks through the finish line ribbon, and receives a gold medal around her neck is a motivated individual. The taste of success is an excellent motivational factor. This is the same in business as in athletics and any other area of life. Be sure to reward employees who are high achievers frequently and sincerely to ensure their continued success.

Ability

Employees with greater skills are more likely to perform better and to feel better about the job they are doing. For this reason, training is crucial to motivation. Perhaps the most pervasive misconception about training is that it is only for new employees. Not at all! Jobs that remain the same over time are few and far between. Consequently every employee will benefit from continuing training. Even experienced employees need to continue their skills development. Some managers place an employee alongside another worker who has the skills that the first employee is supposed to learn. These managers may not understand what is wrong when performance problems arise. Training is one of the most important parts of supervision, and it is always time well spent. Do not hesitate to involve yourself in training, for all employees and at all stages.

Equipment and Environment

Equipment or facilities can contribute to employee motivation. You cannot expect an employee to do the job correctly without having the proper tools. This may be a difficult problem to spot. For example, an employee having difficulty understanding a particular computer program may be reluctant to admit the problem, or may develop a way to get the job done without using the software. An employee who has been trained with a specific piece of equipment may never consider how a different machine might affect productivity. Part of your supervisory duty is to stay alert to physical changes that employees might not consider or believe possible.

Ownership

Employees are motivated by a sense of ownership, which well-run performance management systems provide. Relaying a feeling of ownership does more than retain employees; it also draws the kind of employees you want to keep. Setting clear job descriptions, communicating how the employee's performance will be judged, and offering incentives like stock options lead to such ownership.

If employees know what is expected of them and fully understand the standards by which they will be judged, they will feel ownership of job performance. Employees feel more empowered to get the job done, and more in control of how well that job is done.

One clear way to communicate ownership is through incentive programs that include stock options or profit sharing. In addition to giving each employee the option to literally own a piece of the company, this kind of reward based on the financial well-being of the company motivates the employee. This is particularly successful with smaller companies. Offering a small piece of the company is a benefit, even if salaries are more generous from bigger companies. The feeling of team spirit this inspires is often appealing to potential employees.

A successful example of communicating ownership is Springfield ReManufacturing Corporation (SRC). The engine remanufacturing company was bought by a group of employees in 1978 and CEO Jack Stack, along with his collection of owners and employees, has grown the business by developing new ventures based in part on feedback from his employees.

This company has grown from one nearly broken enterprise to a collection of businesses with combined revenue of more than $120 million today. The reason is that everything is shared among all employees: victory, agony, defeat, all the profits (or lack thereof) that come as a result of the company's ventures. The system, called "The Great Game of Business," emphasizes company-wide sharing of information and employee ownership. This means letting the employees have access to income statements and balance sheets and helping them understand what it means to them and the organization.

The company's main strategy is to identify one problem to solve each year and focus on solving that problem. Performance appraisal, incentives, and compensation are geared toward this issue, which creates a team atmosphere of working toward a common goal and also increases productivity by giving everyone a concrete focal point on which to concentrate. The idea is to focus on improving the problem in one year, as well as looking for ways that decisions will affect the company's future. This system is similar to one Benjamin Franklin followed, though on a larger scale. Franklin kept a list of the things he wanted to accomplish and improve, and each week he would concentrate on one thing from that list. The theory is that when one is focused on a task, the task gets completed in the most efficient way.

"I feel like I'm an owner of the company," says Michael Suarez, an SRC employee, "primarily because we all are. We each have, in our own personal account, shares of SRC stock." (Online MSNBC article, "Giving Employees a Stake in the Outcome," 1999)

Stock ownership is part of the SRC ownership model. Clear communication of the value of the stock and the rules for buying and selling are key to these types of programs. Quantitative measurements that communicate how the company is doing should be easy to find for all employees, and preferably prominently displayed to increase interest and motivation.

Not only the company's financial standing, but also the people's attitudes speak to the success of SRC's Great Game of Business. SRC is known for being an employer of choice within its community as well as in the manufacturing industry.

For more information on SRC and The Great Game of Business, see Tom Olivio's previously mentioned article at *http://www.msnbc.com/ news/229381.asp*.

Retention

Another benefit of performance management systems is employee retention. Performance management systems nurture employees and show them that their managers and the company they work for are interested in making the working relationship succeed. By being available and openly communicating, the chances to catch employee dissatisfaction at an early stage greatly increase. Managers have the chance to improve or remove things that are troubling the employee, if that is in the best interest of the company and the employee.

WHO'S USING PERFORMANCE MANAGEMENT SYSTEMS?

In recent years, an increasing number of companies, including Lucent Technologies, Inc. and Chase Manhattan Bank, have turned to more effective performance management systems.

People in all positions, from entry level to managerial, are increasingly busy, with more demands on their time. The key to success, as well as survival, is working more effectively. An employee who understands the individual goals as well as the goals of the whole company is more likely to be motivated, productive, and able to achieve the desired goals and objectives.

LUCENT TECHNOLOGIES, INC.

Lucent called their implementation of performance management the "Valuing People" program, which by its name suggests that they understand the importance of the employee. The system is based on core goals set at the company level, which all Lucent employees are encouraged to adopt. Lucent's team-based performance management system has led to increases in quality, a rise in customer satisfaction, and hefty cost reductions.

The company reviews employee satisfaction via survey. The rating of employee satisfaction from internal surveys jumped from 30 percent in 1989, before the program was implemented, to 70 percent in 1997 after the program began.

It took a while for employees to be convinced that management was taking their concerns seriously. Changes in how executives were compensated and replacing the standard yearly review with periodic reviews based on individual progress toward previously selected goals helped to relieve these concerns.

Two important elements of Lucent's program are that employees are encouraged to monitor their progress and discuss it with their manager throughout the year, and that managerial scores are openly published, which allows for collaboration and shared learning among managers. For more information on Lucent Technology, Inc.'s implementation of performance management, see "The Continuing Search for Performance Excellence," The Conference Board, Inc., 1998.

CHASE MANHATTAN BANK

Chase Manhattan Bank is one of the largest, most successful, and most profitable banks in the United States. When Chase Manhattan makes a move, other banks are close on their heels to follow. A business this size can easily lose sight of the individuals working to make that kind of success possible, but if it does the success will not continue for long.

To ensure that this success continues, Chase uses performance management classes to help managers perform at the top of their ability, and in the best interest of the people they supervise. According to Acumen, a performance solution company that provides automated multirater development tools and consulting services, Chase Manhattan Bank has been using their ACUMEN Leadership Work*Styles* program for several years. This program is offered to first-level and higher-level managers. The beginning class includes self-assessment and small classes for reviewing assessments of Chase-specific managerial practices. The class for higher-level managers includes feedback from direct reports as well as a self-assessment.

The positive results from these training programs over the last several years have inspired Chase to implement a number of initiatives to build up a more widely adapted performance management process that includes feedback for all employees.

THE OFFICE OF MULTICULTURAL INTERESTS (OMI)

OMI uses a system called *The Productive Edge* for their performance management needs. The Office of Multicultural Interests is part of the Australian government, employed by the Executive Director, Department of Contract and Management Services in Australia; it is relatively small with seven employees. When it was decided in 1998 that the group needed to monitor performance, *The Productive Edge* system was selected as the most appropriate for their purposes. The system was chosen to allow the seven employees to monitor their performance inexpensively, thereby not eating away the funds the group had saved for pay increases for the employees.

All seven employees participated in the process, which is based on a series of short interactive workshops through which the team develops its own productivity standards. The group attended workshops to understand the need for measurement, set up a system for measuring performance, select the means of measurement, and decide upon a rating scale for these measurement points. The seven employees selected criteria such as the ability to improve performance, relevance, ease of data collection, and the degree of control the group had over the indicator.

In the six months that OMI has been using the system, overall productivity has improved. One key aspect of OMI's work involves coordination with Australia's Department of Prime Minister and Cabinet, called Ministerial Correspondence. This Ministerial Correspondence, key to the operation of the Department of Prime Minister and Cabinet, has historically faced a challenge to deliver on time, but has done so since the implementation of the system.

For more information on OMI's performance management system, *The Productive Edge*, see Case Study No. 39, Office of Multicultural Interests Team Based Key Performance Indicators, *http://www.sengai.com.au/c39-omi.htm*.

COMMUNICATION IS THE KEY

Communication and feedback allow clarification of company or supervisor expectations and allow the employees to contribute their perspectives on the importance of given aspects or responsibilities. Open lines of communication offer a means by which these two views can be aligned, benefiting both the employees and the company.

Job descriptions should clearly outline each position's responsibilities. Definite parameters eliminate most misunderstandings about who should be held accountable for what. Certain aspects of a job description are nonnegotiable, but these elements still need to be discussed with the employee so that they are recognized as requirements.

Communication also encourages the employee to see the manager in a coaching role. Managers' regular feedback about the employees' day-to-day performance is one component of successful performance management, and sustained communication will reap additional benefits. With constructive two-way feedback, an employee is more likely to ask for or suggest new goals when the old ones have been met or exhausted. This keeps the employee reaching and growing rather than coasting or stagnating with obsolete objectives.

When problems arise, an employee is more likely to seek advice from a supervisor who is genuinely interested and actively involved. Aside from the obvious benefit to the employee, this also keeps you, the supervisor, attuned to the workings and problems of the workplace and encourages you to stretch your own problem-solving techniques.

Employees are stimulated by challenge, and having a sense of investment in the objectives further facilitates a sense of employee ownership. Most people rise to challenges rather than shirking their responsibilities.

All of this clear and ideal communication is most likely to be realized within the framework of an organization that respects the performance management process and supports 360-degree feedback. The term *360-degree feedback* refers to positive and constructive performance review and evaluation that goes up, down, and across the organization, helping to inform and improve all personnel levels within a company. It is the process of evaluating employee performance by soliciting specific job performance information from an employee's coworkers, managers, direct reports, and customers. (See more on this in Chapter 3, Ongoing Monitoring and Feedback.)

Without the support of all levels of an organization, even the best theoretical performance management system cannot be truly effective. The organizational culture is a seminal element of the performance management system.

NURTURING EMPLOYEES AS RESOURCES

Performance management operates on the idea that employees are valuable resources, and that often the potential of these resources goes untapped. An open environment in which employees can set and achieve what they perceive as meaningful goals fosters dedication and excellence. Willing employees can pursue their projects and advance themselves and, by extension, the company. This process helps to reduce turnover and saves the expense of training new employees. Employees who believe that the company is making the effort to help them develop professionally are less likely to look elsewhere. Employees with the potential to advance are noticed rather than overlooked, to their advantage as well as the company's.

CREATING MORE EFFECTIVE MANAGERS

Managers and supervisors who are involved in performance management become more effective. Communication about obstacles and challenges encourages cooperation and creative thinking and ensures that supervisors are involved in the process. Also, with expectations and goals clearly established up-front, managers spend less time troubleshooting and negotiating with employees. In addition, a manager's ability to develop a staff can serve as a performance indicator to the manager's supervisor.

CONSEQUENCES OF POOR PERFORMANCE MANAGEMENT

Failing to implement a system of standard-setting, ongoing performance monitoring that includes 360-degree feedback, and successful performance appraisals, risks damaging employee trust and motivation, which can lead to losses in productivity and profit for the corporation.

Properly implemented performance management systems help employees to feel involved with their own career improvement, as well as the future success of the company. When performance management is mishandled, employees may feel as though they have little influence on their own future with the company or with the company's performance. With this attitude, employees will not be motivated to increase skills or productivity.

PITFALLS TO AVOID WHEN IMPLEMENTING PERFORMANCE MANAGEMENT SYSTEMS

Unfortunately, some managers misunderstand performance management as another burden on their schedule or an additional source of administrative paperwork. Do you find yourself having any of the following attitudes?

"I shouldn't have to babysit my employees."
While some managers may recognize that troublesome employees
need extra attention, they are often reluctant to spend time supervising excellent workers. However, even self-motivated employees
benefit from guidance. After all, they are the future of the company.
With your direction, their performance may increase or they may
be willing to tackle additional or more complex responsibilities. If
you just smile and say nothing, these employees may never grow
out of their current comfort zone, a limiting factor in the growth of
the organization.

"My employees know what to do."
Do your employees know what their manager expects of them?
How? Do they understand how and where their responsibilities fit
into the larger organizational goals? Any project needs a beginning
plan, and feedback is critical to true progress. How are job descriptions created? Who is responsible?

"I don't have time."

Managers who believe that supervising and guiding their employees takes too much time is probably not training or supporting those employees properly. Proper supervision should not put a strain on a manager, or make the manager feel overburdened. The problem may also stem from higher levels of the hierarchy. If a manager's supervisor is not managing properly, and the manager feels constantly watched, then the feeling of having no time can be caused by the pressure of being micromanaged. The people who work under you are your greatest resource. Taking the time initially to train them to do their jobs properly will save a lot of time, money, and frustration for everyone later on.

"Employees shouldn't get too comfortable."

A manager with a perpetually tough front may be trying to ensure that employees stay on track through fear tactics. Rigidity does not guarantee results. In fact, employees are likely to work more diligently for an even-tempered, respectful supervisor than for a harsh or explosive one.

"You get what you pay for."

In management, as elsewhere, money only goes so far. Higher pay rates may attract employees with more education or more experience, but these attributes do not guarantee the best results. The best employees are those with knowledge, skills, and a sense of commitment to their work.

"I don't like confrontation."

Confronting a problem in the workplace is never a pleasant experience, but ignoring it simply allows the pattern to continue. A comprehensive management training system is one of the best ways to reduce this commonly uncomfortable situation. Instead of anticipating a battle, prepare yourself for a healthy challenge of the status quo, which is likely to lead to better results for both individuals and the department. Think of these encounters as opportunities to advance individuals' growth or redirect them to consider more appropriate career options. Since a comprehensive performance management system does not leave room for many surprises, the probability of an unexpected confrontation is greatly reduced.

"Do as I say, not as I do."

Any time managers take the approach that their titles allow exemptions from standard rules, guidelines, policies, and procedures, they strain the relationship between employee and boss. Whatever your privileges, perceived or actual, employees still look to you for the model of the expected behavior, and if your actions and statements are not aligned, others will naturally follow your example instead of your instructions or learn to resent you and disregard or sabotage your management efforts. Role modeling is a small yet critical part of a manager's job. Nuances may have dramatic impact upon employees.

"They've got it all."

A shiny office building, a new computer, and a hefty holiday bonus are only partial components of motivation. Few people in the workforce are motivated by material gain alone. Even if profit is the primary goal, social interaction and personal appreciation are powerful influences on daily performance. The respect and attention of a supervisor play no small part in this dynamic.

Unlike the traditional employee review, the performance management system is a process for both the employee and the manager. What, then, is your role as a manager? You need to have a solid understanding of the system and then be able to guide your employees through its steps.

ROLE OF THE EMPLOYEE, MANAGER, AND COMPANY

Successful performance management systems mean employees, managers, and the company must work together. The system works beyond the personal level, beyond even the departmental level, and is aligned with company goals to maximize the benefits to employees, managers, and the whole corporation.

First, corporate goals are shared with all levels of the organization. The manager understands the goals of both the corporation and the employee and can encourage those that are in line with each other. Employee goals should be set with knowledge of the corporate goals. Striving to meet these specific goals aids productivity.

ROLE OF THE MANAGER

In general, the manager should keep the employee involved at each step along the way, constantly give and be open to feedback to be aware of the employee's true performance and needs, and alleviate any potential tension at appraisal times.

Feedback! Feedback!

Give specific feedback throughout the year based on notes you take. Avoid falling into the trap of random evaluation or evaluating an employee in a periodic appraisal meeting based on most recent performance.

Set Goals

Work with employees to set career goals that are consistent with their skills, knowledge, experience, and the interests of the company.

Be Open

Be open with employees about possibilities for advancement and possible blockades. Tell employees about job openings throughout the department or company. Show the employee that you are as interested in his or her career development and well-being as you are in your department's success or the success of the company.

Encourage and Assist

Encourage and assist employees to get help with problems at work, from peers with experience in the trouble areas, other managers, or external resources, including books or other sources of information.

Focus
Encourage employees to focus on clear, specific, and attainable career goals, and share your knowledge and experience with them.

Challenge
Challenge employees to help them grow. Be aware of what employees can handle and push them to excel within their range and eventually to expand their capacity. Consider delegating one of your own responsibilities that is appropriate to the employee's classification and development. Act as a coach and a model for employees.

Understand Duties
Understand the employee's job description and day-to-day job duties by maintaining open communication with employees.

Set Expectations
Set expectations with the goals of the company in mind; be sure that goals do not get in the way of job performance.

Decide How Meetings Should Run
When it is time to hold a periodic performance appraisal meeting, decide how the performance meeting will be run, including length, whether to use forms or essays, and whether you will also fill out a form.

ROLE OF THE EMPLOYEE
The employee's role is to communicate the perception of the job to the manager and to work openly to agree on expectations, goals, and standards.

ROLE OF THE COMPANY

The company's role is to set company-wide goals and to evaluate the managers to see that they and their reports are in line with these goals. Management should communicate to managers that appropriate measurement standards help employees establish and achieve their goals. Motivation and productivity increase when well-established goals are linked with positive and publicly shared feedback.

The company's most important role is to support management in all performance management tasks. A company-wide understanding that such efforts are a worthy expenditure of time is crucial to the success of performance management systems.

Chapter 2

Understanding the Job and Setting Standards

You people are telling me what you think I want to know. I want to know what is actually happening.

—Creighton Abrams

Chapter 1 explained the basics of performance management: what it is, who is using it, why they are using it, and what happens if such a system is implemented poorly or not at all. Use this chapter to begin implementing a performance management system. The first step in implementing performance management is to fully understand the employees' jobs, so that appropriate standards can be set for the employees.

AWARENESS OF JOB DESCRIPTIONS AND JOB DUTIES

The first step to effective performance management is awareness. How do you keep on top of what your employees are doing without adding a few hours to each day? Communication and availability are the answer. Do not keep yourself locked behind closed office doors. Make it a point to periodically check in with employees, and you make it easier for employees to come to you. Comfort leads to communication.

Here are some suggestions that will help you understand the ins and outs of your employees' jobs, while keeping yourself visible and accessible.

◆ **Take a walk through the department each day.** Observe your employees and answer their questions. Varying the time of day when you take your walk allows you to observe a wide range of situations.

◆ **Spend 10 minutes sitting with or otherwise observing one employee per week.** This is an excellent chance for you to see the employee at work. Make the employee you visit comfortable when you stop by, recognizing that some employees may feel singled out or embarrassed by your attention. This is an opportunity for positive feedback and for catching problems that can be noted and hopefully corrected on the spot.

◆ **Institute a regular meeting or reporting mechanism.** Design a system that allows employees to connect with you and discuss their jobs without the pressure of a formal performance evaluation or issues of compensation. Let the employee know that you are there to answer questions.

You must be in touch with your employees to know whether and how they are doing their jobs. Knowing the job description for each employee is essential to this point. In addition to being aware of their overall responsibilities, you must also be familiar with their daily routines. This does not mean that you need to know who drinks decaf and who takes sugar, but understanding what happens in an employee's normal day is essential.

Perhaps more important, awareness facilitates approachability. Effective managers must be capable of interacting with employees. If employees perceive the manager as aloof, they will not willingly come to the manager with questions and concerns, and any input offered by the manager is likely to be discounted. Such distance, perceived or real, stands in the way of true dialogue.

SETTING STANDARDS AND UNDERSTANDING EXPECTATIONS

While job descriptions tell you and the employees what they should do, standards provide a measure of how this can be done. Standards should be determined by employees and management. Whatever language is decided upon, standards are a scale ranging from the best an employee can do to the worst. Standards are life preservers for employees that keep them afloat and steer them toward their destinations. Compensation, which will be discussed in Chapter 5, is tied to these performance standards.

Only when employees truly understand what is expected of them can they do their jobs correctly. Think of players on a basketball team whose team goal is to win. If the point guard understands he must dribble down the court and take the open shot or pass to the open man, and the center understands he must go for the rebound, the team is on the way to victory. If, however, the point guard thinks his job is to shoot every time he has the ball, he will frustrate his teammates, probably cost the team points, and possibly lose them the game.

Companies are more complex than five players on a basketball court, but the concept is the same: Employees, from hourly paid clerks to managers and CEOs, must understand what is expected of them to perform productively. In performance management systems, it is the manager's role to communicate expectations that are in line with the company's goals.

For the basketball team, the equivalent of the corporate goal would be to win the game by scoring more points than the other team. The point guard might interpret this goal to mean "shoot the ball through the hoop as many times as I can." Managers must clearly state expectations to each individual. Continuing the basketball analogy, the coach may tell the point guard that the team should get a good shot off each drive; if a clear shot is not available, then pass the ball.

Taking this example into the business world, let us consider a taxidermy company with the goal of becoming known as the animal-friendly taxidermist. Instead of telling employees to publicize the company's respect for all animals, the director of public relations works with employees to set goals. They decide that the employees should plan one publicity event each month with an animal activist or animal lovers group, or run one public relations piece per month in a national newspaper or large animal interest publication.

STANDARDS FOR EACH POSITION

Standards must be set for each department and individual position. This process is essential for the organization and for each employee. When each department's goals are outlined and each employee's duties are defined, you may be surprised by what you find. Perhaps an employee in engineering has been doing a lot more computer hardware maintenance than anyone realized, and it is time for the company to hire a computer repair person so that this employee can spend more time doing what he or she does best.

Maybe the sales force that was so critical to getting the company off the ground is now verging on superfluous because there are so many standing accounts. The human resources department that seemed unnecessary five years ago might now be a tremendous help to the departmental secretaries who have been struggling to coordinate training and insurance benefits for each division. If you as a manager do not know exactly who needs to do what and why, you cannot communicate the importance of an employee's role. Company-wide definitions and divisions of labor are the first step to increasing understanding and productivity.

Although defined parameters and expectations may seem rigid or cold, both employees and managers benefit from a system that relies on clarity and mutual understanding. As a manager, you will find it easier to hold employees to explicit, documented standards, and your employees will be more willing to pursue an existing goal than one that is suddenly thrown out as "what must be done." Continuous constructive feedback increases the ability to improve performance. Also, employees who are always aware of their standing are less likely to be upset with formal performance reviews or to feel that less-than-ideal reviews are simply excuses to avoid pay raises.

INTERCHANGE WORKS TWO WAYS

This increased interchange works both ways. Managers who know their employees' specific strengths and weaknesses are better equipped to advise and support. An atmosphere conducive to feedback allows discussions about productivity to occur outside the consideration of salary rates, and employees who understand the role of their particular responsibilities are more highly motivated to achieve objectives that lead to the success of the organization.

How do you know if your employees understand what is expected of them? Do they know how to proceed under less than ideal circumstances? Employee misunderstanding may have many causes. Perhaps the employee's training was poor or insufficient. Maybe there is no communication (or not enough) between employee and manager. This includes instances in which the manager thinks that communication has taken place when in reality, or from the employee's perspective, it has not. The employee may not receive constructive feedback and thus may be unable to ascertain whether the job is being done correctly. Maybe the employee has no model for professional performance. Here are two steps to take toward ensuring that employees understand expectations.

TWO PHASES OF ESTABLISHING EXPECTATIONS

First, you must identify the job duties. To do so requires four functions:

1. Manager input

2. Employee input

3. Comparison to job description

4. Employee/manager agreement

Most jobs change over time, and employees recognize this. Most are willing to amend the job description provided that their efforts are recognized. However, if either you or your employee does not see the change or the need for change, little progress will be made. Again, communication is essential. Collaborate with your employees to fill in the details of each position's description. You may be surprised to learn what employees think their jobs are—or what they have taken on without you realizing it. In all instances, it is important to be realistic. Start with the basics and add to them cautiously. Defining responsibility is one realm where idealism has no place. Each detail must be linked to the specific objectives of the organization as connected to the position.

Second, once you and the employee have agreed on a set of duties, you can create performance standards. Now that you know what needs to be done, you can establish how to do it. Because performance standards are rarely addressed in the job description itself, this phase requires three steps:

1. Manager input

2. Employee input

3. Manager/employee agreement

How will you determine levels of competence? What is the least a person could do to retain this position? What is reasonably expected, and what would you consider exceptional performance? Be sure that these expectations are in line with the responsibilities of the particular position, and be sure that they are achievable as well as challenging.

Here is a sample rating system:

Performance Scale
Best: The highest level of performance possible. Every goal set was met on agreed-upon deadlines, and the quality of the work was excellent. Additional initiatives were taken and completed beyond set goals.
Good: Every goal set was met on agreed-upon deadlines, and the quality of the work was acceptable.
Average: The majority of goals with highest priority were met on or close to agreed-upon deadlines, and the quality of the work was acceptable.
Below Average: The majority of goals were not met on or close to deadline, and/or the quality of work was not considered acceptable.
Poor: No goals were met on or close to agreed-upon deadlines. Other problems (that is, attitude issues) were observed that affected work quality, or the quality of the work of others.

After responsibilities and expectations have been established, move on to set goals and objectives. Like expectations, goals must be clearly in line with the tasks and abilities of a given employee and the needs of the company. Guidance does not take the form of arbitrary goals. Any objectives must be logical and beneficial not only to the employee but to the department and company as a whole.

Working together with the employee increases the probability that the employee will want to achieve those goals. It also allows employees to stretch their objectives further than you might have suggested. If you simply hand down goals, an employee may assume that his or her abilities are limited to the list given. Employee input may show you areas of interest or ability that you were unaware a person possessed.

Check to be sure that these goals are in line with your employees' duties. A constructive goal must be one that assists rather than hinders performance. This seems obvious, but it is easy for a supervisor to present a goal that requires such effort to attain that other aspects of an employee's job may suffer. If a library cataloger has a goal of

30 books per hour, he or she may be able to attain it, but the error rate may increase to an unacceptable percentage.

Most employees want to be successful and to advance in the workplace, even if they are uncertain about exactly where to go or how to get there. As a supervisor, it is important for you to be aware of immediate personal and departmental objectives as well as each employee's long-term vocational hopes. Will acknowledging future advancement hinder the employee's work here and now? Not likely. In fact, the enticing idea of moving into a dream job often provides incentive to contribute and learn more. The supervisor's role is to help define the road map for the employee to follow.

INVOLVING THE EMPLOYEE

It is important that employees fully understand the standards that are established. The standards will provide the groundwork for feedback that occurs continuously throughout the year. Documenting the standards in writing will make them clear and explicit.

You can establish performance standards without employee involvement, or work directly with your reports. Working with employees may make getting their support and cooperation easier, and it also may help them to achieve higher performance. If you do decide to involve employees in the process, you may want to speak with each employee individually, or work in groups if particular job duties are performed in groups. You may even involve other managers if a particular employee works on projects outside your department.

If setting standards is a collaborative effort, but you as the manager have the final say about the standards, be sure that the employee fully understands and accepts the final standards. To ensure a truly successful performance management system, standards should not be dictated blindly from the top down. At times it may be necessary to make slight changes or additions to standards, and these edits should be communicated to and accepted by the employee.

THE MEETING TO SET PERFORMANCE STANDARDS

Before a meeting to set standards begins, you should be sure that each employee understands what you mean by performance standards and what they mean to the employee (that is, a measure by which he or she is rewarded with advancement, opportunity, and compensation). Ask for questions at the beginning of the meeting to be sure that everyone is on the same page. Then describe the process you will follow, including the fact that although you are all working to develop these standards, you, the manager, will decide upon the appropriateness of the standards or have the final say.

For this meeting, employees should have copies of their individual job descriptions. Although you won't make a standard for each job item, understanding the essence of the employee's job is necessary to set standards. During the meeting be clear about which specific levels of performance merit which rating. For example, you may tell a salesperson that making 10 sales per week merits a rating of *average* or *agreed target*, five sales would be *below average*, and 15 would be *above average*. The exact wording is up to you, but the employee must clearly understand what the rating categories mean.

PUT STANDARDS IN WRITING

Once standards are agreed upon, they should be written down in clear and specific language. Standards should be described concretely in terms of deadlines, budget limitations, customer satisfaction, and accomplishments outside the normal scope of the job. Be reasonable.

Do not set superhuman standards. Be clear about any prerequisites that must be completed before a task is started, such as taking/passing a programming course or other tasks that the employee or someone else must finish before work can begin.

Beyond the specifics of the employee's job are standards for general on-the-job performance, such as organization or delegation. These should be part of every employee's standards and should be in line with the company's goals.

In summary, standards should relate directly to the employee's job duties. Be clear in the language you use, and try to be as objective as possible, building in goals that can be measured quantitatively.

Include standards for specific job requirements and for traits important to the organization as a whole, as determined by the company's goals.

CHECKING YOUR STANDARDS

Here is a list of six criteria your standards should live up to:

◆ **Realism.** Be aware of setting the bar too high. Employees may just walk right under it. Set realistic standards for minimum and outstanding performance.

◆ **Challenge.** Do not set the bar too low either. Employees need something to reach for.

◆ **Specificity.** After reading your standards, the employee should know exactly which actions will warrant which ratings.

◆ **Objectivity, not subjectivity.** Use measurable items in standards, such as quality and customer satisfaction.

◆ **Consistency with the company's goals.** Standards should reflect the goal or goals of the company.

◆ **Clarity.** Use clear language to ensure that employees understand what they must do.

Chapter 3

Ongoing Monitoring and Feedback

Giving is receiving. When our attention is on giving and joining with others, fear is removed and we accept healing from ourselves.

—Gerald Jampolsky

ONGOING MONITORING OF PERFORMANCE AND 360-DEGREE FEEDBACK

Once a position's goals and standards have been defined, the next step is to determine how these objectives can be evaluated. If you know that your library catalogers need to average 20 full entries per day, then you have a quantifiable goal. A cataloger who falls short of this requirement needs assistance, and because the position has a standard and defined goal, the cataloger is less likely to resist guidance and training. Incorporating performance standards into job descriptions enables managers to exercise greater authority in regulating employee output. It also ensures that employees understand what is expected of them, which may reduce resistance to supervision and constructive criticism.

FEEDBACK: THE MOST CRITICAL COMPONENT

The continuous process of performance management is what will shape and guide employees' behavior. Do not underestimate the value of feedback, and make the effort to keep track of employees' actions and feelings about the process. Feedback allows employees to communicate perceptions of their standings. Employees can assess their level of competence as well as hear your opinion. Constant and honest feedback fosters growth and helps employees to learn what is and is not productive.

Feedback is perhaps the most critical component of any working relationship, and it plays an integral part in effective performance management. What comes to mind when you hear the word *feedback*? Do you perceive it as a euphemism for criticism from above? Too often, both employees and their supervisors feel this way. Feedback may be defined as "information about past behavior, delivered in the present, which may influence future behavior."*

Employees need to cultivate a sense of their own worth as individuals in the workplace. Your praise and reinforcement are important to employees who look to you for a gauge of their efforts. Making a contribution and seeing the potential for growth are important aspects of employee satisfaction. Beyond reinforcement, your willingness to pitch in on difficult matters or to provide tools and guidance for unusual or everyday problems makes a difference to employees.

Open communication is invaluable in encouraging and guiding growth and enhance performance. This is true for managers as well as employees. It is important to remember that *your* performance may need some management of its own! Managers and employees alike need the same type of feedback and performance management to grow and excel at their jobs.

FEEDBACK MUST BE A TWO-WAY STREET

Feedback is the responsibility of both the manager and the employee, because both benefit from clear and ongoing communication. A study conducted by the U.S. Air Force in 1993 showed that 58 percent of people who received written feedback said it improved their performance. More than 90 percent of subordinates and superiors agreed

*Seashore, Charles, and Edith Seashore. *What Did You Say? The Art of Giving and Receiving Feedback*. North Attleborough, MA: Douglas Charles Press. 1992.

that feedback is positive. According to Icy Lee, Chief of the Evaluation Procedures Section, Air Force Military Personnel Center, "The primary purpose of feedback is to improve performance and professionally develop personnel to their highest potential. Performance feedback is the single most effective means for changing behavior."*

Feedback informs employees of how they are doing and allows both manager and employee to catch problems immediately, before they evolve into larger problems. Feedback, both positive and constructively critical, motivates the employee to continue the positive behavior or to improve. Lack of feedback can cause employees to be confused or hesitant about job duties or to continue poor habits. This causes motivation to deteriorate and can cause a ripple effect throughout departments and organizations.

IT'S PART OF OUR NEW PROGRAM TO ENCOURAGE FEEDBACK

---

*Cournoyer, Tammy, TSgt. "Performance Feedback Is Important." *Air Force News* and web site *http://www.af.mil/news/Jun1995/n19950622_658.html*. June, 1995.

You can provide feedback informally and casually, set up structured meetings, or schedule written communications for regular feedback. When there is a problem or a concern, however, feedback must be immediate to be effective, and you should not wait until the regularly scheduled time.

Giving feedback to solve problems is important, and positive feedback is equally important. People respond well to positive feedback, particularly when it is given in public. This infuses employees with confidence and makes them more likely to continue the positive behavior.

BEHAVIORAL FEEDBACK
Monitoring performance and providing feedback based on an employee's specific behavior are central to performance management. The employee must feel comfortable giving and receiving feedback and must trust the validity of the feedback. To gain this confidence and trust, you as the manager must have plenty of quantitative evidence to support your feedback.

Behavioral feedback tends to be accepted more easily because it measures observed behavior related to performance standards agreed upon by the manager and employees rather than judging individual personalities. Employees do not feel attacked when the evaluation is based on specific actions, behaviors, and outcomes, particularly because you have made efforts to ensure that the employees understand and accept the standards against which they are judged.

GUIDELINES FOR GIVING BEHAVIORAL FEEDBACK
It may be helpful to keep certain guidelines in mind when delivering feedback, particularly if you are new to this type of communication. First, be specific and timely when delivering feedback. Include specific

examples of the behavior you observed and give the feedback as close to the observed event as possible. When you are speaking with employees, ask for their input before giving your interpretation of the event. For example, if you notice an employee leaving early on certain days of the week, hearing the explanation from the employee may uncover a legitimate reason. Both good and poor performance have consequences, and you should discuss these with your employees to increase motivation. Be aware of making promises or sounding as if you are threatening the employee. Finally, make sure employees understand that your intention is to help them become more successful through this feedback.

If you deliver positive feedback, a crowd is OK, sometimes even beneficial, if the employee is not shy. If the feedback is not positive, keep it behind closed doors. Either way, you should know your employees well enough to know how they will react in each situation and to act accordingly.

TAKE NOTE OF THE DETAILS

You must be observant to be a successful performance manager. Notice the specifics of an employee's job function as they relate to performance. To observe the details, you must be around. Getting into the habit of noticing and recording details will help make you comfortable with a more personal and involved type of management. Be careful not to be in the way, however. Observing means just that. Provide positive feedback or constructive critical feedback by all means, but do not fall into the trap of micromanagement. Also, be sensitive to employees who feel that you are watching them too closely. Talk to employees and let them know what you are doing. This will ease their minds and reduce possible stress.

By paying attention to the specifics of an employee's job, you will have a stockpile of information to help this employee reach the goals you both have set. This will prove invaluable for you and the employee throughout the year and during any formal evaluation processes.

Examples of statements including specific observed details and generalities:

◆ *That presentation lacked direction. You need to work harder.*

◆ *Your presentation did not give a clear idea of what you were intending to communicate because you didn't choose your topics carefully enough or make it a point to tell the audience exactly what you were there to discuss.*

While the first statement tells the employee that something is wrong, it is not specific enough for the employee to do anything about it. The second critique is more useful. The employee knows that more time should be spent thinking about presentation organization and selecting and communicating the key points of the presentation. As a general rule, to improve performance, ask employees to complete a specific action, rather than to change a broad or vague behavior.

When you give feedback routinely, employees are more likely to be confident in what they are doing and to perform effectively. Share performance-related information with your employees throughout the year. Discuss and record goals as they are accomplished and set new goals. Listen to employees' requests to expand their knowledge or improve skills through classes or training. Take the time to discuss accomplishments, training needs, and any problems or concerns. If there are performance problems, schedule meetings at regular intervals for the purpose of providing feedback on performance. This practice will ensure that you address issues promptly and foster a problem-solving dynamic between the performance manager and employee.

If a serious performance problem is encountered, such as harassment, substance abuse, or selling confidential information, consult your manager as well as human resources or personnel before taking any steps.

EXAMPLES OF EFFECTIVE FEEDBACK

Too Vague	Specific and Effective
You've done a great job this year. (Although the employee will be pleased at the positive comment, he or she will have no concept of what behavior to repeat or continue.)	*I appreciate how you've met every deadline for designing each chip you worked on, and helped us by speaking with customers when problems or questions came up. Your work with customers brought us two additional sales worth $1 million.* (Not only does the employee know what behaviors were appreciated and deemed positive, he or she also understands their direct impact on the company.)
I think you need to improve your writing skills. (This statement is vague and does not tell the employee what the specific performance problem is.)	*This report is too long by at least five pages and the main points of sections 1 and 3 are lost in paragraphs filled with unnecessarily large words. How would you like to enroll in a business writing course to help you become more concise and precise in your writing?* (The employee has a clear idea of the problem and an idea of how, working with the manager, it can be solved.)

Whether feedback is scheduled, impromptu, positive, or constructively critical, it must be from all directions to be successful. This means 360-degree feedback, both positive and negative, in all directions—up, down, and across.

WHAT IS 360-DEGREE FEEDBACK?

The process of 360-degree feedback is the evaluation of employee performance by soliciting specific job performance information from an employee's coworkers, managers, direct reports, and customers. The concept has been around (perhaps often disguised under other names, such as multipersonnel rating) for 20 years. It has been used extensively in corporate America for the past 10 years. Personnel Decisions, a Minneapolis consulting firm, designed its first 360-degree feedback evaluations in 1984 for Cray Research. The Center for Creative Leadership, based in Greensboro, North Carolina, has been using 360-degree feedback questionnaires on consulting projects for more than 20 years.*

The majority of Fortune 500 companies now use some form of multiperspective feedback as input to employee performance reviews. Some of this popularity stems from recent corporate restructuring or layoffs. Companies need to know who the good managers are, as well as the good employees.

This kind of feedback provides an opportunity to learn about an employee's performance from direct reports, peers and employees in other departments, customers, and the individual him- or herself.

---

*Maynard, Michelle. "Evaluations Evolve from Bottom Up: Workers, Peers Rate Managers." *USA Today*, August 3, 1994.

This all-around feedback is especially useful because it combines feedback from people who have firsthand knowledge of a person's performance from a wide variety of perspectives.

Managers, supervisors, and employees alike have found 360-degree feedback to be very effective in improving employee performance. Because feedback is gathered from multiple sources, employees find the results more compelling than traditional evaluations based on a single supervisor's or manager's perspective. Most managers find it is a good tool for grading difficult areas, like conflict resolution, and for learning how others see the employee.

Seeing other points of view helps employees understand strengths and weaknesses and can change behaviors dramatically. Employees are likely to get more feedback than if they were evaluated solely by a manger, and this input is likely to be something that the manager would have overlooked. This type of all-around feedback helps management to see how managers are working with their employees, and helps to determine promotions or new assignments. Also, knowing that he or she will be evaluated by peers, managers, reports, and customers can change the way an employee relates to people. It is customary to be on best behavior with those above you, but some people may not extend the same behavior to others in the workplace. This type of feedback system eliminates selective positive behavior practices.

Some companies currently using this type of feedback include AlliedSignal, The Limited, the Strategy Forum at ATT Network Systems, Ford, TRW, Xerox, and Boeing.

ONE MODEL FOR 360-DEGREE FEEDBACK

One way to implement 360-degree feedback is to start by using the job description and performance standards established by the manager and the employee. The manager can use this information to establish a performance survey and an agreed-upon group of reviewers. The team can be picked by the employee and approved by the manager, or the two can collaborate on the selection. A good-sized team would be about a dozen peers, customers, and supervisors from within and outside the department who have direct knowledge of the employee's work.

Once the participants are selected, each will fill out and return the anonymous evaluation, and fill out and return his or her own evaluation as well. When the results are in, the manager can summarize the evaluations and bring the employee in to discuss the results. Depending on the results of the evaluation, the manager and the employee may agree upon training, courses, or conferences to help improve strengths or eliminate weaknesses. For example, The Center for Creative Leadership offers week-long feedback programs, where results from coworkers in each employee's home office are combined with face-to-face feedback. (*www.centerpointsystems.com*)

Sample 360-Degree Feedback Form for Manager
The following sample 360-degree feedback form was excerpted from the web site of the Center for Employee Development (*www.centerpointsystems.com*), an organization that provides managers and supervisors with information, tools, and services for employee development and the 360-degree feedback process.

Category	Question
Communication	Communicates changes in methods and/or work assignments clearly and promptly?
Communication	Communicates honestly and constructively?
Communication	Shares information openly and candidly?
Customer Focus	Committed to the satisfaction of internal and external customers?
Customer Focus	Responsive to customer and employee requests?
Customer Focus	Treats both internal and external customers with fairness, respect, and integrity?
Leadership	Energizes others to accomplish their business objectives?

Leadership	Expects and encourages performance from others?
Leadership	Leads by example?
Leadership	Recognizes and rewards good ideas from others?
Quality	Carefully reviews any work before it is submitted?
Quality	Makes suggestions to improve quality and productivity?
Quality	Sets standards to achieve high-quality results?
Teamwork	Involves others in discussions of how to achieve team objectives?
Teamwork	Receptive to suggestions for changing or improving the way work is accomplished?
Other	What do you like best about working with this person?

IS 360-DEGREE FEEDBACK ALWAYS RIGHT?

Many have found that 360-degree feedback works best in team-based organizations or other work environments where employee cooperation and trust are high. Knowing that one is being scrutinized by peers and others can cause tension, even when evaluation forms are anonymous. Often people find it easier to ignore negative feedback that comes from the boss because he or she may not work closely every day with the individual. However, if the feedback comes from peers and others who work closely with a person, the feedback has more meaning.

Anyone who participates in a 360-degree feedback evaluation, including managers, should be trained on the rating scale that is being used, on what the information is to be used for, and on how to rate objectively and constructively.

Implementing 360-degree feedback requires putting in the time to learn about the concepts and tools available to make the process successful. The system is different from the traditional management model, and if an organization is not willing to accept the change, the system will not work. When implemented correctly, these types of feedback systems can actually save time and be more accurate due to involvement from others.

When implementing a 360-degree feedback system, steps should be taken to ensure that the system is not abused by letting personal feelings, good or bad, get in the way of fair evaluations. It is also important to keep the process from becoming or being perceived as a popularity contest. Anonymity should help employees who feel uncomfortable giving unfavorable reviews, but the real challenge is to change people's thinking from punishment or reward to "how can I help my coworker or manager to do a better job or improve upon the good job already being done?" This attitude can only be communicated if it comes from the top.

It may not be wise to use the information from a 360-degree feedback evaluation for compensation or incentive purposes. If employees know that they are affecting someone's raise or bonus, it throws tension into the process and could distort results. This technique may be better suited to identifying which skills need improvement and perhaps indicating when training would be beneficial. In the future, as 360-degree feedback systems become more advanced, and means to eliminate or significantly reduce slanted responses improve, more companies may consider basing compensation on 360-degree feedback results.

MAKING 360-DEGREE FEEDBACK WORK

First, teach employees how the 360-degree feedback process works. You can do this by asking your employees to evaluate you. You will also gain trust and acceptance this way. This also may give you an idea of what kind of training the group needs in evaluation practices/ techniques.

When setting the standards for evaluation, you must consider the company's goals. Standards must be in line with an individual's and a corporation's visions for the standards to have any meaning. For example, a manager works for Company A, which values teamwork, and that manager has expressed a feeling of isolation at work that he would like to improve. The manager goes through the process of being evaluated and finds that he is a bit controlling and tends to shut out other people's ideas. The manager and his boss agree that solving this problem would benefit both the manager and the company. The manager's boss then works with the manager to set up a program to help. With the manager's assistance, the two can create a program, perhaps one that includes a seminar and a one-on-one session with a professional management coach. By taking personal and corporate goals into account, the manager can work to improve areas that are a priority.

According to AlliedSignal, 1,800 out of 4,500 managers (40 percent) at the company have gone through 360-degree evaluations. Through the reviews, the company learned that all its managers needed help in communicating with employees and encouraging teamwork. As a result, the company is focusing on these issues, including training. "We weren't meeting employees' expectations," says Peter Mercer, Allied's vice president of organization and management development. "This is a safe way to tell them [managers] where they need to get better."[*]

You may be surprised by how your peers and employees view you, and by the influence of your own negative or positive behaviors on others. A person who considers herself a shrewd businesswoman and an organized and efficient manager may discover that her employees view her as cold and unfeeling. Someone who finds it easier not to hand out compliments on a regular basis may find that his employees perceive him as someone who does not care, or who

---

[*]Maynard, Michelle. "Evaluations Evolve from Bottom Up: Workers, Peers Rate Managers." *USA Today*, August 3, 1994.

is displeased with employee performance. On the other hand, a manager who feels for one reason or another that he is not meeting his employees' needs may discover that he is well liked and considered to be a good boss. In essence, it is hard to guess what people think or feel, and asking them is the best way to know the truth.

Beware of inflated evaluations as a manger. Try not to pump up your evaluation or shoot too low. Think about your strengths and weaknesses, drawing on concrete situations experienced on the job. The well-thought-out evaluation is the most helpful.

When evaluations are in and it is time to work on the areas that need improvement, be creative. Solicit help from others who are strong in those particular areas. Set up mentor relationships or teams of people who can help each other in particular areas.

STARTING 360-DEGREE FEEDBACK
WITH THE INTERVIEW

The techniques used in 360-degree feedback are also an excellent way to hire. You should use the same standards for hiring that you use to evaluate your employees. It is also a good idea to mention that the company uses 360-degree feedback and explain a little about the system. This way, if the employee is hired, he or she already has an idea of how the organization works.

USING SOFTWARE APPLICATIONS
FOR 360-DEGREE FEEDBACK

A good deal of administration is required for the 360-degree feedback system of evaluating and monitoring performance. If the company can afford it, software programs are available to help. There are systems available today that include everything from the basics of reporting functionality to a collection of questions you may want to include on your surveys, and many are reasonably priced.

One important note about using software programs for this aspect of performance management or any other aspect, including the performance appraisal, is that the software is only a tool. Do not forget that the most important part of 360-degree feedback and performance management is the monitoring, development, and coaching of employees to meet goals in line with their own objectives and those of the company.

Before even considering software, make sure other, more critical pieces are in place. The trust of employees and the alignment of the system with the organization's values are absolute prerequisites to implementing a 360-degree feedback system. Once there is adequate support from management, you are ready to think about purchasing a software program.

At this point, consider what you need the software to do. For example, you may want to compare information you collect with your department only or with many departments. You may want the ability to have anonymous evaluations or the ability to track evaluations. You can also determine how often you track data. Make sure you are clear on why you want the software and what you want it to do.

After you determine what you want, look at your resources. Consider how much time and money you have to spend. The total system cost includes the price of the purchase as well as the cost of administration and training time to get everyone up to speed.

When you are clear on the reasons why you want the system, what you want it to do for you, and what resources you need to get the system running, you are ready to shop for the right tool for your business situation.

According to research published by *HR Magazine* (December 1998), in an article titled "Comparing Features with Needs" by N. Elizabeth Fried, Ph.D, CCP, there are three major criteria that a 360-degree software application should meet in order to be considered for testing. The program should be purchased without added consulting services or fees, it should run on a PC, and the vendor should provide the entire program and all documentation for your testing purposes. The study found four programs that met these criteria:

◆ CorporatePulse–PulseTools

◆ CompStar Appraiser Plus 360

◆ 20/20 Insight GOLD

◆ Intelligent Consensus

For detailed information on each of these programs, consult a print copy of the magazine or view the detailed comparison of these 360-degree software packages, "360-Degree Vendor Comparison," available at *HR Magazine Online, http://nefried.com/360/360gold-shootout.html.*

WHY MANAGERS NEED FEEDBACK, TOO

The basis of the 360-degree feedback system, integral to performance management systems, implies that everyone, including managers, needs feedback as much as employees. With 360-degree feedback, evaluations include peers and reports, not only supervisors. This is often an overlooked part of management systems.

Feedback benefits everyone, including the manager. Feedback from peers, employees, and customers lets the manager know how they are doing. Often the further one rises up an organization's ladder, the less feedback one gets. Responsibility for subordinates, departments, or entire businesses can, to the detriment of the manager, make it easy to lose sight of one's own performance.

Asking for Feedback

Asking for feedback can help build trust between management and employees and can nurture the manager's continuous improvement. The manager can act as a model for the rest of the team, department, or business. Modeling certain behaviors is usually more effective than demanding them.

Feedback from the people you manage, as well as customers, can be very telling. Problems and weaknesses, as well as strengths, that you or peers would not pick up on are often unveiled when employees or customers rate the manager. However, it is important that the employees feel comfortable, and not threatened by, evaluating their managers. For feedback to work, it must be honest and trustworthy.

Gathering feedback from bosses, peers, employees, customers, and others actively involves them in the process and empowers them. A 360-degree feedback environment can especially improve the support you get from those you manage. Support is more likely to come from those who feel respected and those who feel their manager values their input enough not only to listen to it but then to act upon it.

MONITOR FEEDBACK TO STAY ON TRACK

As a manager, you must make time to monitor and supervise your employees. It sounds simplistic, but managers may get caught up in so many administrative details that they neglect their primary function—supervising their employees. You cannot manage effectively if you lose the sense of your employees' routines and projects. Take a few minutes to break down your day. How much time do you spend coaching? How much of your day is spent interacting with employees? How much is consumed by administrative duties? The scales should tilt more toward coaching, or showing employees through example, and interacting.

Here are some ways to help build supervision into your schedule by monitoring the feedback you give your employees.

USE YOUR CALENDAR

Write the employee's initials in for any day you give feedback. On Thursday, check the week's results. If you have missed anyone, be sure to give that person feedback before the week ends. Do not, however, give empty compliments just to meet your quota. The idea is to make a habit of giving employees regular, sincere feedback.

BROWN BAG LUNCH

Once a week, have a brown bag lunch with an employee. Use this time to catch up on recent events and get the employee's perspective on how things are progressing.

FEEDBACK EVERY DAY

Give feedback to at least one employee each day. This should be positive feedback or constructive feedback, and it should be sincere and not forced. Sticking to this schedule and this discipline will exercise the feedback muscles.

BE VOCAL ABOUT GOOD WORK

People like to be praised, from children in grade school to your employees. It is of no use to give empty compliments, but when rewards are truly merited, publicly praise employees with positive feedback.

TECHNIQUES FOR GIVING FEEDBACK AND MONITORING PERFORMANCE

Coaching and amending are excellent tools in the performance manager's tool belt that help with monitoring and enhancing employee performance. *Coaching* is a way to show, rather than tell, the employee the type of performance the manager would like to see. *Amending* is a technique to help when particularly poor performance or other performance problems arise. For both coaching and amending, the key is to focus on improving performance or assuring good performance on a new task or skill by focusing on the performance.

COACHING

In addition to being a supervisor, you must work to become a coach. In contrast to mentoring or leading by example, being a coach requires you to prove your competency in the daily logistics of your business. Anyone can tell a clerk that customer service is of utmost importance, but a coach can show the clerk concrete, step-by-step ways to satisfy a customer. An effective coach moves beyond theory and authority to practice and expertise.

Coaching is a natural progression from open communication. You may find it the most difficult aspect of performance management, because coaching must be tailored to the specific needs of individual employees. As a coach, you must make your interest and concern visible, and you need to develop a nonthreatening atmosphere conducive to 360-degree feedback.

Like feedback, coaching often carries only negative connotations, but the fact is that coaching is essential for star employees as well as difficult ones. If you have a self-motivated and capable employee, coaching can engage him or her in new projects and at higher levels of involvement. Most people willingly rise to a challenge, and raising the bar for employees eliminates vocational stagnation.

Employees who seem to be "weak links" in your work chain will also benefit from coaching. A regular stream of feedback reminds these employees that their performance is monitored and lets them know where they stand at all times and that you, the supervisor, are actively involved. Your attention to their performance will show you which behaviors or skills need improvement, and you can work with the employee to facilitate these changes.

CONSTANT INVOLVEMENT FROM ALL LEVELS

Constant involvement from all levels is the key ingredient of coaching. It shows that help and reinforcement are readily available while encouraging effort. The individual emphasis encourages ownership of a given activity, and this feeling of personal investment in a task leads to increased involvement and concern for the outcome.

When possible, arrange situations in which employees receive immediate feedback or can determine their own levels of performance. This allows employees to control and adjust their performance while still in progress, rather than reflecting on possible changes after the fact.

There are two types of coaching: *field* and *sustained*. *Field coaching* tends to be spontaneous and dictated by the situation. It might be used with any employee to solve an immediate problem. *Sustained coaching* requires more time and planning, frequently in response to an identified and already determined challenge that the employee faces.

FIELD COACHING

This form of coaching tells employees what they have done correctly, instructs them in specific situations, is immediate and brief, and is characterized by one-way communication from the manager to the employee.

In field coaching, simply approach the employee and state what she has done well or what she needs to do. Try to associate directions you give with a performance objective.

> Example: *"Kim, why don't you finish that strip of negatives so you meet your 12 scans per day goal?"*

SUSTAINED COACHING

This type of coaching is a way to address a recurring performance problem by determining its cause and then examining ways to change it. Some characteristics of sustained coaching are that it

◆ commends outstanding work.

◆ is time-consuming.

◆ involves two-way communication.

Sustained coaching is a more detailed process, but is more in line with true performance management, particularly 360-degree feedback. The following 10-step process outlines one approach to sustained coaching.

1. **Set up a meeting with the employee.** Hold the meeting within a short time after setting it up. Within the hour is ideal, whereas waiting half a day is too long. You do not want the employee to have time to worry or become defensive.

2. **Meet privately.** If you don't have your own office space, ask to use someone else's or find a spot that will be free from interruptions.

3. **Start with the basics.** Tell the employee why you called the meeting. Do not sound accusatory; instead, state that you are concerned about a particular behavior or pattern.

4. **Offer supporting evidence and cite specific examples.** This ensures understanding and assures the employee that your concern is based on fact.

5. **Compare the noted behavior with an established performance standard.** Remind the employee of the previously established expectations and show the relationship between these standards and the employee's actions.

6. **State your feelings about the behavior.** Keep it short. "I'm concerned about this" or "I'd like to see a change" will suffice. Coaching is not meant to be a release or gripe session for you.

7. **Ask what the employee thinks.** It is important for the employee to understand that this is a cooperative and helpful process—not punitive. Until you know what the employee thinks of the behavior, you cannot continue productively.

8. **Reach agreement.** Unless you agree on the situation, it is unlikely that the employee will be willing to change the problem. This step may be the most arduous, but it cannot be bypassed if you truly wish to address the issue. Reaching agreement can easily take more than one meeting.

9. **Discuss the behavior.** You cannot effectively change a behavior or situation you do not understand completely.

10. **Establish direction.** Collaborate on a list of possible actions to change the behavior or situation. Using these options, draft an improvement objective particular to that employee and that situation. Involve the employee in finalizing the objective. This represents your agreement on a direction and outcome for solving the problem.

SAMPLE COACHING CONVERSATION

Consider the following conversation. How does Lydia do?

Francine:	You wanted to see me?
Lydia:	Yes, come in, Francine. Have a seat.
Francine:	Thanks.
Lydia:	I noticed that you have been late with your weekly reports for the past three weeks.

Francine:	I know I've been a little late, but only a day or two, and I don't want to rush them.
Lydia:	I realize that. In fact, other than the late reports, I have no complaints about your working habits. It's still important that you adhere to the standards we've set up, and that includes getting your reports in on time.
Francine:	What about Henry? He turns his reports in on time, but he does them without any effort.
Lydia:	Everyone is responsible for his or her own job duties, and if Henry is not meeting his goals and standards, then Henry and I will work that out.
Francine:	I understand.
Lydia:	You definitely have the capability and skill to advance, so it would be a shame for a relatively minor problem to hold you back. I know you're a hard worker, so I have a lot of faith in your ability to discipline yourself to get your reports in on time.

What do you think? It seems that Lydia does a good job of presenting the problem objectively, but it comes across that she is concerned about the behavior. She handles Francine's question about another employee professionally. On the down side, she does not actually ask Francine for her thoughts on the subject of getting her reports in late, and there is no specific goal set. While a "talking-to" of this sort may be enough for an employee who wishes to avoid trouble, further steps may be required in the future.

AMENDING

Amending is also a form of coaching, but it is specifically used for troubled employees or for those who have a poor pattern of performance due to a serious problem. What can lead to poor performance? High stress, difficulty with coworkers, personal problems, and sickness are just a few factors that might influence performance. Although some of these are outside the manager's control, it helps to keep an eye out for potential problems, so any help that can be given comes early.

SPOTTING A TROUBLED EMPLOYEE

These are some common behaviors that may indicate a troubled employee, although they vary from person to person.

◆ excessive tardiness

◆ frequent early departures

◆ frequent absences

◆ late returns from lunch or break

◆ numerous personal phone calls (incoming or outgoing)

◆ decline in productivity, or apathy

◆ accidents in the workplace or elsewhere

◆ failure to complete required duties

◆ hostile behavior

◆ extreme sensitivity

◆ mood swings

◆ crying

◆ disruption or withdrawal

Most troubled people exhibit overt behavior changes. These can be either complete reversals of usual characteristics (a reliable employee coming in late or missing work) or exaggerations of typical behavior (a quiet employee retreating into total isolation). Overt behavior is more than just an occasional mistake or a passing mood; it develops into a pattern and affects performance.

Unlike coaching, which deals with isolated or relatively routine performance problems, amending refers to extended patterns of overall poor performance. Because such problems often result from personal problems, you may find yourself in a difficult position as a manager. Although you have a vested interest in the employee's well-being, you also cannot—and should not—attempt to tell employees how to handle their personal lives.

The key to amending is to focus solely on the employee's performance. Do not become involved with the employee's personal problems. If your organization has a human resources department that may be able to offer assistance or provide references or an employee assistance program, make this information known to the employee. However, your role is to attend only to the job performance itself.

First, identify the performance problem to the employee. Explain exactly how you want the behavior to change. Also, state the possible consequences of not changing the behavior. Making a threat is inappropriate, but an accurate assessment of potential results is entirely in line. As with all performance problems, documentation is essential both for illustrating the problem to the employee and for protecting you against claims of unfair treatment. With amending, more of the responsibility for change lies with the employee. You may continue to coach on specific issues, but the employee's decision is key to the situation. If the employee decides not to correct the performance, you must be prepared to follow through with the stated consequences. It is unfair to the company and to other employees to allow inappropriate behavior to continue.

Using the performance management system reduces the likelihood of negative surprises at the time of the appraisal. However, even when the employee knows that the appraisal will be less than favorable, the information must be presented in a coherent and professional manner.

TIPS TO IDENTIFY AND RESOLVE PERFORMANCE PROBLEMS
Use the following guidelines to get to the bottom of performance problems.

Identify the exact problem. Determine exactly what the problem is so it can be communicated clearly, and identify the employee's specific behavior and actions that should be changed.

(Example: *Applications are not being processed within 48 hours of their receipt. The result is lost revenue. What is the employee doing to cause the delay?*)

Determine if the employee understands his role. If the employee is clear on his duties, then this is not an issue, but you will only know this by first talking to the employee. If there is some confusion, training may be required.

Find out if ability is an issue. An employee may not have adequate ability to perform a task, and if the task is integral to the job, this can lead to problems. If a particular ability, or a set of skills, is an issue, consider an easier or different way that the task can be completed; or change the job requirements by adding and removing certain tasks; or, if there is no other option, transfer the employee or terminate employment.

Consider whether the employee gets adequate feedback. If an employee is unsure of how she is performing, tension and frustration can cause poor performance. If feedback is the problem, try telling the employee specifically what is being done incorrectly. Also remember to praise small successes immediately and often, and give both constructive feedback and praise frequently.

See if work-related obstacles can be removed. An employee's performance problem can be as simple as not feeling he can leave his desk for lunch. If you think there may be a work-related obstacle that could be removed, talk to the employee to see if this is true. Listen to the employee's concerns openly and then evaluate the situation. Remove the obstacle if possible. It is a good idea to be aware of the work environment and habits of your employees in general, even if problems do not seem evident. This can prevent obstacles or uncomfortable conditions from beginning in the first place. If

obstacles exist and are not removed or reduced, nothing else will succeed in changing the performance.

Determine if motivation rather than ability or training is the problem. One reason why an employee may not be motivated to perform well is that the consequences of not doing the task properly are more positive than those of doing the task correctly. If, for instance, not doing the task properly means the employee can leave at 5:00 P.M. each day but doing it correctly means she must stay until 9:00 P.M. with little or no additional compensation or recognition, the employee may opt for decreased performance. If this situation is a possibility, analyze why it is happening, change the consequences, and reward the desired behavior.

Another possibility for lack of motivation causing performance problems is that the consequences of doing the task properly are negative. In this case the manager should again analyze the situation, remove the negative consequences, and reward the positive behavior.

A third reason could be that the consequences of doing the task properly are the same as those for doing the task improperly. In this situation, again determine why this is the case, then create positive consequences for the desirable behavior and negative consequences for the undesirable behavior.

A final possibility may be that the employee has a problem, whether work-related or personal, that is resulting in poor performance. If this is the case, the manager may not be in a position to resolve the problem. What the manager can do is to speak with the employee and concentrate solely on the performance problems on the job.

Chapter 4

The Performance
Appraisal

Flatter me, and I may not believe you.
Criticize me, and I may not like you.
Ignore me, and I may not forgive you.
Encourage me, and I will not forget you.

—William Arthur Ward

The performance appraisal itself is the part of the performance management system that parallels the old employee review. Even here, though, you will find that certain changes will boost the positive impact and long-term value of the appraisal procedure to the employee and the company.

SAMPLE CRITERIA ON WHICH TO BASE PERFORMANCE EVALUATION

◆ Attendance/Punctuality

◆ Deadlines

◆ Cooperation with coworkers and supervisors

◆ Receptivity to suggestions

◆ Time management

◆ Equipment use

◆ Prioritizing of tasks

◆ Quality/Accuracy of work

◆ Problem solving

◆ Creativity/Originality

◆ Communication: verbal and written

◆ Technical/Professional skills

SAMPLE JOB DUTY AND PERFORMANCE STANDARD

Job Duty	Performance Standard
Complete insurance forms for patient records	accurately and legibly, by the end of the office day
Answer incoming calls	by the third ring, identifying office and self
Schedule appointments	according to patient's schedule and as soon as available
Type letters to patients	completing at least five error-free letters per day
Monthly billing of accounts payable	to be recorded and sent out by the fifth of the month

TWO STEPS TO THE PERFORMANCE APPRAISAL

The two steps to the performance appraisal are the preliminary verbal appraisal and putting it all in writing.

PRELIMINARY VERBAL APPRAISAL

The preliminary verbal appraisal is the first step for you and the employee. This meeting allows you to review goals from the past period and to talk about the current standing of the employee. Also, be sure to touch on possible future objectives.

PUTTING IT IN WRITING

The next step is to put the appraisal in writing. Working together, you and the employee can transfer the discussed aspects of those three areas—past goals, current standing, and future objectives—into a written format. Modifications to job descriptions are usually the easiest way to slide into a performance management discussion.

There are several ways to incorporate the written element of an appraisal. The manager and the employee might work together to create an essay-style review of past, present, and future, meaning a few paragraphs of prose describing the events, or instead might choose to use a standardized form.

If the choice is a standardized form, fill out one yourself and have the employee fill out one separately. This is called the dual-form system. Discussing similarities and differences in the ratings often creates an easier entry into true conversation than a supervisor-only review method. This is the only way to maintain the 360-degree feedback mechanism.

The dual-form system also paves the way for verbal discussion of the jointly created written review. The final recap needs to address not only goals achieved and set but also the perceptions of each party regarding the process. In addition, you and the employee need to create an action plan to attain the next goal. The action plan is arguably the part of the process with the most impact. This sets the stage for future development and increased employee value.

BRINGING IN A THIRD PARTY

With certain employees or in specific situations, it may be necessary to bring in a third party, such as a human resources professional, to facilitate the process. Third party assistance might be necessary when

◆ addressing an employee who is belligerent.

◆ informing an employee that his job is in danger.

◆ dealing with issues that are personality-related.

◆ assessing a problem between manager and employee.

◆ enforcing company policies or procedures.

UNDERSTANDING COMMON RATING TRENDS

There are several common trends that a manager's ratings may follow. Do you see any of these tendencies in your performance appraisals?

Central Tendency

You rate practically every employee as average in almost every way. This often indicates that you have not gathered sufficient information and are taking the safe way out.

Unfounded Generosity

Although rating employees consistently high regardless of actual behavior may seem like a good way to maintain pleasant relations, this tendency often allows problems to progress to a point at which they are impossible to handle. Also, an employee fired over performance issues may be able to use your consistently positive reviews as evidence in an unlawful discharge lawsuit.

For example, an employee is fired because of irregular and inconsistent performance. If your performance reviews did not include examples of failure to comply with workplace standards (arriving on time, prompt returns from breaks and lunches, attendance at mandatory meetings), the employee could easily claim to have been fired on illegitimate grounds. Without sustained historical documentation of the problem and attempted solutions, you have no way to counter this accusation of wrongful discharge.

Unwarranted Harshness

If you think that withholding high ratings is motivation for your employees to work harder, you may be unpleasantly surprised. Keep in mind that positive behavior reinforcement is a powerful way to encourage people to continue on an upward path. Honesty is the key. If the person is doing poorly, do not sugarcoat it. But remember, no surprises.

Short-term Memory

Your perspective may be skewed if you base your annual review ratings only on the employee's behavior in the past month. Conscientious documentation throughout the cycle is the best way to combat this supervisory pitfall. See the section on Keeping a Performance Journal for more information on ways to remedy the short-term memory pitfall.

Halo/Horns

An employee works magic with even the most disgruntled customers. Because her service skills are so effective, you assume a rating of excellent across the board and naturally rate other characteristics highly. This is a prime example of the halo effect (the horns effect is its opposite, when one undesirable trait is assumed to be indicative of an employee's entire performance). Wearing these appraisal blinders will not help the employee to improve in problem areas.

ENCOURAGING EMPLOYEE PARTICIPATION

Encouraging employee participation in the performance appraisal process helps to mitigate many of these potential imbalances. Employees are unlikely to allow their achievements to go unrecognized, but most people are also willing to identify areas in which they can improve. Maintaining open communication and an environment conducive to 360-degree feedback helps to even the playing field throughout the performance management process, not only at the time of the formal appraisal.

What can you as a manager do to ensure fair and accurate reviews? Document, document, document!

KEEPING A PERFORMANCE JOURNAL

Even the best memory fades eventually, and everyone is likely to recall most clearly what happened most recently. Keeping a performance journal for each employee helps to counteract these human flaws and enables you to be more informed and objective when preparing for a performance review. Few companies currently make full use of performance journals, and because they seem novel to many supervisors, some are reluctant to try them.

COMMON EXCUSES FOR AVOIDING PERFORMANCE JOURNALS

"I have an excellent memory. Recording is a waste of my time, because I'll remember anyway."
Even if your memory is superb, you are still likely to be more influenced by recent events than earlier ones. Maintaining a running record of all events will help you to balance your opinion when the performance appraisal comes up.

"This is for managers with big departments. I only supervise a few employees."
All supervisors can make use of documentation, no matter how many employees they manage.

"It's too time-consuming. There are other tasks that need my attention."

Nothing is more important than helping your employees improve their performance. If you set aside a specific time each week for documentation, you can get it done quickly. You might even find that it encourages you to organize your own time more effectively. The exception is dramatic events, which should be recorded immediately for purposes of accuracy.

"Employees won't like it. They'll feel like they're being spied on."

Performance journals document all performance, good and bad. All information that you record on employees should be open to the employees, and knowing that their performance is noted may encourage marginal employees to excel. In addition, supervisors who document are likely to evaluate employees more favorably because recent errors will not overshadow good decisions and behavior of the past.

"Putting things like this in writing can't be good. What if it comes back to haunt me?"

The opposite is more likely to be true. As long as you keep the proper information in your performance journals, the documentation can actually protect you. What is it appropriate to include? Read on.

MATERIAL TO INCLUDE IN PERFORMANCE JOURNALS

When the performance appraisal is due, you need to have at least the following information available to you in the performance journal:

◆ employee's length of employment with company

◆ positions held and date of last promotion

◆ educational and experiential background

◆ level of technical skills or degree of training

◆ current projects and status thereof

◆ employee's relations with coworkers, clients, and others

Begin with the basics. If you have an employee's résumé, start with that. If not, at least maintain a list of the positions or titles that the employee has held within your company, accompanied by dates and salary information.

Example:
Kelly Johnston at Quick Pix One-Hour Photo Lab
Sales clerk: June 1996 to February 1997, $6.50 per hour
Technician: February 1997 to December 1998, $7 per hour
Assistant manager: January 1999 to present, salaried at $22,000

The following sections detail things to update or record in your journal over the course of the year.

UPDATE YOUR JOURNAL ON A REGULAR BASIS

It is a good idea to update the journal every week or every other week. Unusual incidents or situations should be recorded immediately in order to have the most accurate rendition. To avoid potential problems later, have the employee involved read your account to ensure its accuracy. That signature can protect you from accusations later. If this seems like too much bureaucracy, you may have employees sign only in sensitive situations.

Example:

June 10, 1998.

Customer requested copy of portrait on print-to-print machine. Kelly explained store policy that no copies be made of pictures that appear to have been taken by a professional unless customer has signed release form or can otherwise show that permission to duplicate has been obtained. Customer became angry and abrasive, shouting at Kelly and other employees. Kelly offered to call a manager, but customer refused and walked out of store, leaving the portrait. Customer returned the following day for the photograph and told manager that Kelly had been rude and disrespectful. Manager conversations with Kelly and the two other employees present convinced manager that Kelly had handled the situation to the best of her ability. No disciplinary action was taken. Signatures were obtained from manager and employee.

Keep track of absences. Tardiness or extended lunches and breaks, as well as overtime worked and offered, should be recorded. Available training programs, as well as those attended, should also be included.

Example:

November 3, 1998: Kelly returned 15 minutes late from lunch.
January 15, 1999: Training program for APS film processing attended by Kelly and lab manager.

Document specific activities. Aside from obvious documentation like sales figures or productivity rates, for example, make note of the time spent on certain activities, such as sales calls or paperwork. Record any particularly good or bad decisions and any feedback that you have received from coworkers or clients about the employee in question. Note the progress of the project, and how the employee has contributed to that progress. Project descriptions and the progress made on them can offer insight to expediency, efficiency, and effectiveness.

Example:

Average of $1500/week in camera sales
Approx. 5 hours/week spent calling customers with late film
10 hours/week for inventory and ordering
March 3, 1997: complaint from customer that prints were not ready at promised time and Kelly did not offer discount or other compensation.
July 14, 1998: letter from customer thanking Kelly for special assistance on son's wedding photos.

Make note of any verbal warnings or other disciplinary actions. These records can be used to support further action or low appraisal ratings.

Example:

March 15, 1997: After missing the Feb. 4 and March 8 mandatory lab meetings, Kelly was warned that another unexcused absence would result in disciplinary action.

Note quality of employee's work, not personal impressions. It is acceptable to include your impressions of the quality of the employee's work, provided your other documentation supports the judgment you offer. Other personal impressions should not be included. They are inappropriate, unnecessary, and likely to reflect poorly on you rather than the employee. Remember, no secrets. Any formal written documents must be reviewed by the employee if they are considered part of the personal file.

Example:

Kelly's interest in the technical aspects of film processing appears to be genuine and a true motivation for her to learn more about the business. She frequently asks questions about chemicals and mechanical maintenance and keeps a running list of issues to address with the technical representative from our equipment supplier. Although her understanding of the lab is thorough and she is usually quick to help customers, she is not always willing to explain her actions or knowledge to other employees. Getting Kelly more involved with training new workers would benefit all involved and might encourage new employees to approach her with their questions.

Avoid inappropriate comments. Some issues are not entirely clear-cut. For example, while it is inappropriate to comment on an employee's fashion sense, it is fitting and important to note that an employee who is required to wear a uniform does not properly care for it. Similarly, commenting on personality traits is generally off-limits, yet an employee whose character others find difficult to work with may need to be approached. In each case, keep your comments linked to a performance objective.

Example:
Inappropriate:
Kelly is cold to other employees and needs to be more sociable in the workplace.

Appropriate:
Kelly's knowledge of procedure and policy can benefit her coworkers. Because employees are uncertain whether she can be approached in the lab, perhaps a formal question-and-answer session could be established at the weekly lab meetings.

THE PERFORMANCE APPRAISAL MEETING

Employees traditionally dread performance appraisals, and while the comprehensive performance management system may not alleviate that fear entirely, it can reduce tension associated with a review. Effective performance management includes the employee at each step along the way.

During the preliminary verbal appraisal, discuss the entire process with the employee. Restating the goals set at the last interval and assessing the current standing of these objectives assures that you and the employee are starting in the same place (or on the same page). It also provides an opportunity to discuss future goals and the company's culture before putting anything in writing.

The written appraisal requires joint effort. Together you will review prior goals, evaluate performance, and establish future objectives. The employee's involvement in the construction of this document contributes to the sense of ownership. A follow-up verbal discussion provides the chance to discuss differences in perceptions or expectations that have surfaced. This offers the employee a chance to ask questions and raise any concerns, which traditional employee reviews often neglect.

Allowing for employee input not only leaves the employee with a better feeling about his or her role in the appraisal (not to mention the department or company), but it may reveal problems and opportunities that you would not have recognized otherwise. For instance, take a look at what Richard discovered thanks to his policy of having employees assess the amount of time spent on each aspect of their jobs.

Richard: On your time analysis sheet, I see you've esti-
              mated your troubleshooting/problem-solving time
              at 40 percent of the total. Is that accurate?

Caroline: I think it is.

Richard: That seems like a high percentage for a pro-
              grammer. Are you having problems with the
              system? Or with your computer itself?

Caroline: Oh, no. At least, no more than is expected. It's
              just that a lot of the other programmers come to
              me when they have questions or get stuck. I don't
              like to brush them off and send them to you or to
              tech when I know I can help them.

Richard: Well, I appreciate your willingness to help. Still, it's
              not your job to troubleshoot for other programmers,
              and their problems shouldn't take up your time.
              Let me ask, are the questions always different, or
              do you find yourself answering the same things
              over and over again?

Caroline: Hmm. A lot of them are the same, or similar
              enough that it seems like they should be easily
              figured out.

Richard: What would you think about helping me design a
              training course for the programming department?
              Since you know what questions come up most
              frequently, your input would be valuable.

Caroline: That would be neat. It would be a nice change of
              pace, too.

Richard: Since you noted that you're interested in taking
              on a role that involves more leadership, this
              would be a good opportunity for you to exercise
              your organizational and managerial skills, too.

Caroline: That would be great. Back to the training idea—
                I think the company should also consider creating
                a handbook or manual that addresses the most
                frequently asked questions.

Richard: That's an excellent idea. I think this will be good
                for you as well as the company.

HOW TO PREPARE FOR
THE PERFORMANCE APPRAISAL

Because performance appraisals are relatively infrequent, they may be difficult to prepare for, even for the most skilled manager. Here are tips to help you conduct the process and the meeting as smoothly as possible.

DOCUMENTATION

Document performance with examples both positive and negative throughout the year. If your form uses numerical or otherwise closed ratings, write comments for each set. If your system is lenient, expand on it to serve your needs and those of your employee. Don't hesitate to change or add to an existing form if the alterations give you and your employee a better basis for discussion.

This is where your performance journal proves its worth. Come to the meeting with relevant entries marked by paper clips or Post-it notes so that you can show the employee examples quickly. In addition, mark the entries that show when you have spoken to the employee about the troublesome behavior; this counters any claim that the employee was unaware of the issue. Although a good performance management system ensures that there are no surprises in the performance appraisal, a poor performer might be reluctant to remember past discussions of problems. If you have documented effectively, you can show the employee that the problem was previously identified and discussed; this eliminates any complaints of falsehoods or surprises.

JOB DESCRIPTION

Having the written job description and any standards or goals that have been written on hand provides irrefutable evidence of what is expected.

PRIVACY

Performance appraisals are highly personal and sensitive. Use a private space, whether your office, someone else's, or another reserved room.

DISRUPTION

Do not allow interruptions. The employee deserves undivided attention at this time. Be sure to allow more time than you expect the meeting to take—better to err on the side of caution.

SCHEDULE

Meet as closely as possible to the scheduled appraisal times and dates. If appraisals are to be done every six months, do not wait eight months to get around to the next review. Set a meeting time and keep it. Delays suggest that your interest in the employee's performance is negligible.

PARTICIPATION

Discuss the employee's performance; don't lecture on it. An appraisal is more effective when the employee has invested time and effort into it.

EYE CONTACT

Eye contact equals credibility. Maintaining a connection reminds the employee that you are concerned, not disinterested. Maintaining this visual connection with your employee also encourages immediate feedback. It is difficult to initiate a discussion with a person whose attention you cannot catch.

COMPARISON

Which ratings did you agree on? Where did you differ? Use examples to illustrate your opinions and carefully consider the employee's observations. If the employee brings to your attention a factor you had not considered, simply change your ratings.

LISTEN

Plan to listen more than talk. Do not rush your employees to speak; allow them time to consider carefully the issue at hand. Let silence rule if necessary.

FUTURE FOCUS

Past behavior cannot be changed. What is more important is to improve what actions are to come. Be sure the plan of action is clear, concise, and agreed upon.

IDENTIFY

Both you and the employee are likely to have ideas of what behaviors or actions need improvement or enhancement. Work jointly to create a list of areas to improve and areas to develop.

LIST CHANGES

Simply telling an employee to improve will not help either of you. The more specific you are about what needs to change, the more likely you are to see those changes implemented.

GOALS

Set specific short-term goals. Short-term goals, especially those with visible results, are most likely to encourage action. Tell the employee that once improvement is made on these short-term goals, you will meet again to discuss future goals.

SPECIFY

Choose one area or behavior that will be the first focus for the employee to create an improvement objective and work on changing.

Allow the employee to make the first suggestions. For any action determined, set a deadline or other quantifiable limit.

HONESTY

Explain what needs to change and the probable consequences if performance does not improve. If the employee's job is in jeopardy, say so. This issues a warning, not a threat, and can protect you legally from a discharged employee who may seek retaliation.

SUMMARIZE

As the meeting closes, recap the main points. Confirm the chosen improvement areas. Be sure you both sign this agreed-to summary of job requirements and goals.

POSITIVE

Be positive about the employee's ability to improve. When possible, offer training opportunities. Be sure to present training as an opportunity to solve existing problems and not as a punishment. Both you and the employee must agree that training will be beneficial. An employee who resists additional education is unlikely to get anything out of it. However, if you present the offer with faith that the employee will utilize it and with respect for the ability to do so, most employees will agree to the chance to learn more.

End the appraisal on a positive note. Smile. Shake hands. State your confidence in the employee and your anticipation of discussing the goals as they are reached.

AVOIDING CLICHÉS

Because the employee's perception of your feelings about the situation can have a powerful effect on the way he or she responds to the situation, practice phrasing common concerns and compliments in a way that will truly affect the employee. A trite "good job" is empty praise; letting employees know that you value their individual time management skills or ability to handle several tasks at once makes the praise more personal and concrete.

Here are common clichés that might come up in performance appraisals.

◆ You're not living up to your potential.

◆ I thought you had enough experience in this area to handle this assignment without difficulty. Why do you think you've had trouble getting the work done correctly/efficiently?

◆ You use your time well.

◆ I'm impressed with how you organize your workload. The fact that you finished that last project without any overtime is especially notable.

◆ Your customer service could use some work.

◆ You aren't trying.

◆ You work well with others.

◆ You need to increase your technical knowledge.

◆ Your productivity needs improvement.

◆ You need to prove you can handle this responsibility before I can give you more.

EIGHT QUESTIONS EVERY PERFORMANCE
APPRAISAL SHOULD ANSWER

You can use these eight questions a successful performance appraisal should answer as guidelines to help keep the performance appraisal on target.

1. *What were the previously set objectives?*
   Review the goals determined at the last meeting and assess the employee's progress in meeting them.

2. *Which objectives need more work?*
   Discuss what obstacles have prevented goals from being attained and how such impediments can be overcome.

3. *What objectives have been reached?*
   How did the employee's skills and performance relate to the success of the department and the company as a whole?

4. *What is the ultimate career goal for the employee?*
   Has it changed? Are the objectives reflecting progress toward that aim?

5. *What new objectives can be set for the coming year?*
   These need to reflect both the employee's career goals and the department's or company's goals. What does the employee need to learn to reach these goals?

6. *Where does the responsibility for reaching these goals lie?*
   Reach a consensus on what the employee must do independently and what you will help with or supervise.

7. *Where will the employee begin?*
Not knowing where to start keeps many people from making progress. Determine together the logical first step and all subsequent steps. An action plan gives the employee a distinct path to follow and assists you in knowing what actions to target with field and sustained coaching.

8. *When will you meet again?*
Do not just set up another performance appraisal for six months or a year in the future. Agree to meet in a month or two to evaluate progress to date.

◆

LOOKING TO THE FUTURE

Reviewing what has happened is an important part of the performance appraisal. However, it should not overshadow the other essential element, which is what will happen in the future. Setting goals during appraisal, both short-term and long-term, helps keep the balance between past and present.

SHORT-TERM GOALS

Short-term goals can affect immediate workplace changes and any necessary performance improvements. Setting and meeting short-term goals is often motivating, because results can be seen more immediately, and results motivate.

EXAMPLES OF SHORT-TERM GOALS

◆ Daily entries will increase by 15 percent within three months.

◆ Three customer complaints will be processed per hour.

◆ Brochure designs will be transmitted to customers for approval within five working days of their request.

◆ Employee A in the cataloging department will reduce her error rate to 7 percent before the next performance review.

LONG-TERM GOALS

These are more specific to the employee and her individual expectations. These goals take into account the employee's future career aspirations. By understanding and defining long-range ideals, an employee can learn and utilize skills needed for the future in the current situation. As a supervisor, you can help the employee develop skills that will benefit her in her current position and will enable her to accrue more experience, responsibility, and capability. A worker motivated by a future goal will be a better worker now.

FORWARD-LOOKING QUESTIONS END
THE APPRAISAL PROCESS

To cap off the performance appraisal process, managers should ask the employee questions that are focused on the future. Some examples of such "goal questions" include the following.

◆ What would you like your next job title to be? What do you see as the best path toward that goal?

◆ Are you interested in some of the training seminars available through the company? Are there courses offered outside that might be beneficial to you?

◆ Where will your current career course take you? Is that where you want to be? What are the pros and cons of continuing on your current path?

◆ What long-range goals have you set for yourself? What do you plan for the future? How do you see yourself getting there?

◆ What are the requirements for that future? Do you need to find out more?

◆ Is your present job preparing you for those future goals? How can you lay down the best foundation for what you see as your long-term plans? Is there another path that might be easier or better suited to reaching those goals?

◆ What career changes do you need to make to reach your ultimate goal? Can you feasibly make those within your current position?

◆ What elements of the position are appealing? How could these areas be used to develop a career path?

HANDLING NEGATIVE REACTIONS

When an appraisal is less than ideal, some employees react poorly. Here are some basic suggestions on how to handle such a situation.

IF THE EMPLOYEE CLAMS UP

Resentment or hostility may cause an employee to avoid talking to you altogether. You do not need to make an effort at small talk in an attempt to smooth things over. Often, the silence will dissipate on its own, but if it continues, speak to the employee frankly. Request a discussion that will enable you both to put the issue behind you and resume normal relations. Keep in mind and remind your employee that performance appraisals include 360-degree feedback. His or her comments will be included in the appraisal report, so encourage the employee to prepare written commentary or to otherwise respond to the appraisal.

IF THE EMPLOYEE WALKS AWAY

Some people recognize that they are unable to face an issue and choose to remove themselves from the situation rather than lose their temper. You may ask the person to please stay so that the conversation can be finished. However, do not try to restrain someone who turns his back on you. It is better to let the person leave and then return to the issue later, when both sides are calm and prepared to face the situation. Investigate why the person walked out. Were there any surprises for which he was unprepared? What could you have done to avoid these surprises? How can your preparation be reconciled with the issues at hand? Be sure to contact your supervisor or human resources to inform them about the situation—and maybe ask for advice.

IF THE EMPLOYEE SHOUTS AT YOU

Do not respond in kind. Keep your speech calm and firm, and do not appear intimidated. If the employee continues shouting, ask the employee to leave and say that you will pick up the discussion after you are both calm. Should you feel physically threatened, call security or a colleague for assistance.

IF AN EMPLOYEE CRIES

Be compassionate, though apologies are likely to do more harm than good (assuming that you handled the appraisal professionally up to this point). Offer tissues. Agitation on your part is likely to exacerbate the employee's embarrassment, so remain calm. Sit and let the person cry—be respectful and wait until he or she is ready. Suggest that you talk about the issue a little later. You might leave the room to allow the employee to regain composure, especially if sending the employee out of the room will put him or her on display to other workers.

SENSITIVE AREAS

With the contemporary awareness of sexual harassment, it is important to keep your performance reviews and appraisals unquestionably legitimate. Any comments, even small talk, should be unrelated to appearance or personal and social activities.

Other subjects can be potentially troublesome as well. Comments regarding family matters, vacations, real estate, or other people in the office may be held against you, legally or personally. Discretion is imperative at these times when many employees are wary or downright hostile, and doubly so when your review is less than flattering. As long as your criticisms are performance-based, you should be in the clear. Focusing on job responsibilities and measurable expectations is the best way to stay on track.

Comparisons among employees are especially problematic. The best way to avoid conflict and keep things on track is by saying, "Let's talk about you, not anyone else." Do not compare the experience, knowledge, or skills of the employee in question to those of anyone else; limit your comparisons to those between the employee's actions and the applicable goals or expectations.

It is also important to keep questions of money out of the appraisal process. Salaries and promotions can be addressed at the follow-up meeting, but the performance appraisal itself should be based on performance issues alone.

ATTITUDE

One of the most awkward issues to address is that of an employee's attitude. Because it is less quantifiable and more personal than many other performance areas, an employee's attitude can be uncomfortable to discuss. Such a situation puts you in the position of reprimanding instead of dealing with the employee as an equal, or it can if you are not careful. Do not treat the employee like a child. State the problem without making a judgment on the behavior. It is best to avoid the term *attitude* altogether, as it immediately sets up a defensive reaction. You and the employee both know that the attitude is the question, but by focusing on behaviors, you eliminate the chance for the employee to complain that you are attacking his or her personality. Use these examples as a start:

Negative Example

Your personality is too abrasive toward your coworkers.

I don't like your attitude.

You'll never succeed with that attitude.

Positive Example

You need to speak more respectfully to your coworkers and your supervisors.

Your behavior makes me think that you resent doing the work that is asked of you (be specific here). If that's not true, how can you change your behavior to reflect that?

You have the ability to succeed and do well. Some of your behaviors are standing in your way. What can you do about this?

Chapter 5

Development and Compensation Programs

If you expect the best,
very often you will get it.

—Anonymous

At this point you understand the concept and benefit of performance management, and you know more about the steps involved in performance management, including feedback and the performance appraisal. The final piece to the puzzle is the development of your employees and selecting the right system to link compensation to performance. In practice, development should happen throughout the performance management process, and compensation should be linked to at least some parts of the performance management system.

DEVELOPING EMPLOYEES' WORK SKILLS

Developing employees' skills and knowledge requires a commitment to learning and working with employees to plan for their futures, with or without the company. Of course you should work on developing employee skills that coincide with company goals because that is a major precept of performance management, but you should also consider the employees' future plans.

COMMITMENT TO LEARNING AND DEVELOPMENT

Keeping employees trained and informed about the latest industry information, technology, and trends benefits your company. It is also beneficial to the employee to continue to grow as the industry or the workforce grows.

You should plan the development of your employees throughout the year. Some companies make this a formal part of the review process. The important thing is to be committed to the development plan, to communicate this commitment to your employees and to follow through. The plan should include training, course work, seminars, in-house mentoring programs, internships, on-the-job training, and any other development opportunities that you and the employees agree upon. These development opportunities should improve the employees' skills based on the standards you set for performance monitoring, the company's goals, and the employees' career objectives.

Once development goals and actions are agreed upon, write them down. This acts as a sort of contract and shows your dedication to the employee, as well as the employee's commitment.

Performance development plans should be considered with the needs of the organization and the needs of the employee in mind. Think ahead two months and then two years and consider what resources your department or business may need at these points in time. Consider what preparation employees will need.

Supporting and encouraging employees will spark motivation, trust, loyalty, and commitment.

CHOOSING THE RIGHT COMPENSATION PROGRAM

While most managers do not have much of a say on this, it is important to understand that there are options available for compensation programs. Management must select the kind of performance measurement and compensation system for the company. Choices include pay for performance, stock programs, profit sharing, or a combination of these.

When selecting a program, each individual business must consider the business's situation, financially and competitively. With these two things in mind, evaluate programs based on specific characteristics. Consider the cost in money and time to administer compared to the value to the business. Also, decide whether the system is intended for short-term or long-term results, for profit or growth. Be careful not to select a solution based only on its simplicity. The incentive or reward program must be in line with the other facets of your performance management system, such as employee motivation and development.

Possible solutions to finding the right compensation program include measuring the company's profit or growth against that of the competition. This requires that the financial information of the competition be accessible and that economic differences truly affect all companies equally. You may decide to set up several incentive plans, setting varying performance standards depending on the economic situation of the company.

Compensation systems can be measured based on the typical earnings per share model, or purely on profit, or on other models, such as intrinsic market value, discounted cash flow, economic value added, and return on invested capital. For these systems to work, however, management must be committed to communicating these concepts throughout the company to ensure that they become an integral part of the performance management system. Though this can be a challenge, it is beneficial to go beyond basing performance on the bottom line because it makes top and middle management, and perhaps even employees, aware of the processes involved to get to that bottom line.

Compensation programs tend to be based simply on the bottom line while performance management systems tend to measure performance using a wider lens (for example, intrinsic market value).

There must be a marriage of these two concepts for a performance management system to work.

EVALUATION OF MEASUREMENT CRITERIA FOR COMPENSATION PROGRAM

The Financial Side

This numerical measure of a company's success measures past performance, summarizing a range of income and balance sheet transactions.

Earnings. Whether it be pre- or posttax, operating earnings or earnings per share, this is the bottom-line figure. Basing compensation on the bottom line for employees other than top executives who directly influence one or more bottom-line figures will not motivate employees, because they will not see the relationship between their performance and the compensation. Open-book companies, which allow all employees to see the financial figures for the company, may be well-suited for earnings-based compensation.

Gross Revenues. Sales figures. This can be deceiving unless considered in the context of the business and the marketplace. The value of a company's goods or services changes depending on whether the company is a manufacturer, a distributor, or a service firm. In some businesses, more must be taken into account than the amount of dollars brought through the door. True sales success is measured when market share is taken from a competitor or new markets are discovered, not just when profits rise due to the rise or fall of the market in general.

Returns. Financial return-ratio measurement considers reinvestment or payout of earnings and whether the earnings objective has been met.

The Functional Side

This measures how goals set by management were accomplished. For example, if the success of the marketing department is based on a mixture of total expenses and perceived customer quality, you must decide their priority and set the standard for marketing performance based on those priorities.

UNDERSTANDING ALL ASPECTS OF THE COMPANY'S STRATEGY

Once the criteria for measuring performance are set, management must determine the features, and this means having a clear understanding of corporate strategy.

The three major parts of corporate strategy are corporate, business unit, and functional area, according to Berlet and Cravens.* At the corporate level, performance measurement should be based on how performance affects the company's products or services and the successful allocation of resources. At the business unit level, performance is measured based on the success of a particular product line or service. At the functional level, performance is based on cost management, completion of tasks, and the efficient handling of day-to-day work.

CORPORATE PERFORMANCE

To evaluate performance at this level, management must decide on measurement criteria, such as stockholder return or comparison with competition, and then rank these criteria in level of importance to the company. Top-level management is compensated based on how they perform in the top-rated criteria categories.

---

*Berlet, Richard K., and Douglas M. Cravens. *Performance Pay As a Competitive Weapon: A Compensation Policy Model for the 1990s.* John Wiley and Sons, Inc. 1991.

BUSINESS UNIT PERFORMANCE

First, determine whether you are dealing with a business unit or a functional area. Cost and revenue are management responsibilities for business units and not for functional areas. Second, decide on the evaluation criteria to measure the success of the product line or service. Use both financial and nonfinancial criteria, such as whether the company or department expanded into new markets or gained market share.

FUNCTIONAL AREA PERFORMANCE

At this level, criteria must be clearly defined for each individual. It is also important that participants in incentive programs at this level not risk other types of performance to meet criteria. For example, if a computer engineer is focused completely on designing X number of chips per week, the quality of the chips may suffer. Another thing to consider is the expense of tracking such performance. The time and money spent in monitoring should not outweigh the value gained by monitoring.

CHOICES FOR PERFORMANCE MEASUREMENT

There are a number of options available for linking compensation to performance.

PERFORMANCE-BASED COMPENSATION

Also called pay for performance, this is the performance management preferred system. See the next section on Pay for Performance. By using a compensation structure that is flexible and performance-based, organizations can motivate their employees to strive for their best performance.

STOCK OWNERSHIP

When competing for talented employees, companies often offer ownership opportunities through company stock. This can be done with private or public companies, and the vesting period for stock ownership varies widely depending on the industry, compensation structure, and individual company.

PROFIT SHARING

Many successful companies use profit sharing to encourage organizational growth. This is one of the best methods of getting employees excited about the company as well as their impact on the bottom line of the business.

PAY FOR PERFORMANCE—THE PERFORMANCE MANAGEMENT MEASUREMENT PREFERENCE

Performance-based pay means that an employee's pay increases as the employee learns more and can contribute more to the organization. This approach rewards cross-training and allows corporations and managers to use their employees more flexibly. This also helps employees by encouraging them to expand their knowledge and learn new skills.

Historically, executives have been involved in performance-based pay programs, receiving rewards for their role in helping the corporation meet goals. Sales teams and some hourly employees also participated in similar incentive programs, and the rest of the employee base was compensated by salaries and wages alone. In the 1980s, pay for performance gained popularity for rewarding other groups of employees while acting as a means of empowering and motivating.

Performance-based pay programs, though certainly of interest, are slow to be adopted, perhaps because of thoughts that incentives can replace management. In order to pay employees for meeting performance goals, those goals must be set and progress monitored. That is why it often works well to match a well-run performance management system with a pay-for-performance model.

The key to the success of such programs is alignment with the company's culture and organization.

For performance-based pay to work you must have

◆ a strong performance management system

◆ full support from the company

◆ trust and acceptance of the employees

Pay-for-performance models can reward individuals based on how they meet their goals and help the company or department meet goals, or the system can reward teams, based on how a group of individuals performed.

Mobil Corporation successfully implemented a pay-for-performance model that included cash and other benefits (such as theater tickets) that were awarded to both individuals and teams based on performance. Two types of cash rewards, one ranging from $250–$2,500 and another reaching up to $5,000, were awarded to individuals or teams whose work increased profit. In the first year of this program, Mobil spent $32,000 on the smaller award and got a $40 million return on the investment. The return on the higher rewards was $18 million on a $19,000 investment.*

OTHER THINGS TO CONSIDER WHEN IMPLEMENTING PAY FOR PERFORMANCE

When implementing pay-for-performance programs or other incentive programs, consider the following three points.

1. Consider the work culture and business values, and beware of off-the-shelf systems.

2. Remember that incentive programs are about the message and motivation as much as the payout of money or benefits.

3. Before implementing pay for performance, determine what goals you are trying to accomplish, establish criteria for measuring performance, and set the amount of payout for various levels of performance.

---

*Hofrichter, David A., Thomas P. Flannery, Paul E. Platten. The Hay Group. *People Performance and Pay: Dynamic Compensation for Changing Organizations.* The Free Press, 1996.

SAMPLE PAY-FOR-PERFORMANCE INCENTIVE PLAN

In this example, at the beginning of each year, executives determine objectives for improving productivity and profit in each business unit. In our fictional company, one business unit's main concern is manufacturing operations. In a second business unit, implementing a new sales force is key. Also, the executives are aware that throughout the year the priorities may change.

To set objectives and design an incentive program in this example, the executives needed to accommodate shifting priorities. Let us say the original priorities were incorporated into a performance profile, which was linked to a payout schedule. During the year, as priorities changed, the CEO added the new priorities and adjusted the performance profile. When it was time to allocate bonuses, the objectives throughout the entire year were reevaluated and the payout schedule was adjusted. This sample system is heavily based on flexibility, and requires ongoing monitoring and adjustment. It requires a little more administrative work, but it allows the company's goals to grow throughout the year, rather than stagnate, and does the same for the manager's and the employees' goals.*

---

* Berlet, Richard K., and Douglas M. Cravens. *Performance Pay As a Competitive Weapon: A Compensation Policy Model for the 1990s*. John Wiley and Sons, Inc. 1991.

Chapter 6

Conclusion

The expert at anything was once a beginner.

—Hayes

Simply put, performance management systems pay attention to people. The company realizes and communicates the value of people resources and of working together. Managers and employees take this message and work together toward company goals. Employees communicate what they think they should be doing, where they see problems with

their own performance or the attention or feedback they get from the manager, and where they want to go in their careers. The manager gives the employee feedback, accepts feedback, and removes obstacles or works out employee problems to ensure productivity.

For successful performance management, the manager must

◆ understand the job duties of the employee.

◆ work with the employee to set standards and expectations.

◆ ensure that accurate, sincere, and ongoing 360-degree feedback is being communicated from peers, supervisors, and customers both to the employee and the manager.

◆ properly prepare for and carry out verbal and written performance appraisals.

Managers must also decide on details of implementation, such as what compensation systems to use and the criteria on which to measure these, and whether or not to use software to help the process. Above all, though, when implementing performance management systems, there must be commitment from the entire company, top to bottom, to make the system work.

REFERENCES

ARTICLES

Alimo-Metcalfe, Beverly. "360-Degree Feedback and Leadership Development," *International Journal of Selection and Assessment*, Volume 6, Number 1, January 1, 1998.

Balakrishnan, Subra. "The Influence of Human Resource Management Policies and Gain-Sharing Plans on Business Performance," *International Journal of Management*, Volume 14, Number 1, 1997.

Booth, Rupert. "Performance Management: Making It Happen," *Management Accounting: Journal of the Institute of Cost and Works Accountants*, Volume 75, Number 10, 1997.

Bracken, David W., Lynn Summers, and John Fleenor. "360-Degree Feedback—High-Tech 360," *Training & Development*, Volume 52, Number 8, 1998.

Burke, Kathryn. "Resources—Practice Management—Managing Staff for Optimum Performance," *Canadian Family Physician*, Volume 44, November 1998.

Carroll, Carolyn, John M. Griffith, and Patricia M. Rudolph. "The Performance of White-Knight Management," *Financial Management*, Volume 27, Number 2, 1998.

Coates, Dennis E. "Don't Tie 360-Degree Feedback to Pay," *Training*, Volume 35, Number 9, 1998.

Collins, Denis. "How and Why Participatory Management Improves a Company's Social Performance: Four Gainsharing Case Studies," *Business and Society*, Volume 35, Number 2, July 1, 1996.

Edwards, Colin. "360-Degree Feedback," *Management Services*, Volume 39, Number 6, 1995.

"Failing to Have a Formalized Appraisal Process for the CEO Is a Breeding Ground for Misunderstanding," *Informationweek*, Number 613, January 13, 1997.

Fletcher, Clive, Caroline Baldry, and Nicole Cunningham-Snell. "The Psychometric Properties of 360-Degree Feedback: An Empirical Study and a Cautionary Tale," *International Journal of Selection and Assessment*, Volume 6, Number 1, January 1, 1998.

Gaiss, Michael. "Enterprise Performance Management," *Management Accounting*, Volume 80, Number 6, 1998.

Garavan, Thomas N., Michael Morley, and Mary Flynn. "360-Degree Feedback: Its Role in Employee Development," *The Journal of Management Development*, Volume 16, Number 2–3, 1997.

Heuerman, Allan D. "Using Performance Management to Energize the Results Act," *The Public Manager*, Volume 26, Number 3, 1997.

Kennedy, Peter W. "Performance Pay, Productivity and Morale," *The Economic Record*, Volume 71, Number 214, 1995.

LaFee, S. "Pay for Performance," *The School Administrator*, Volume 56, Number 2, 1999.

Lepsinger, Richard, and Antoinette D. Lucia. "Creating Champions for 360-Degree Feedback," *Training & Development*, Volume 52, Number 2, 1998.

"Management Techniques—The Performance Pyramid," *Accountancy*, Volume 120, Number 1252, 1997.

Manatt, R. P.; Kemis, M. "360-Degree Feedback: A New Approach to Evaluation," *Principal*, Volume 77, Number 1, 1997.

Massauro, Maureen, and David Westman. "Designing a Systems Approach to Performance Management," *CUPA Journal*, Volume 49, Number 1–2, Spring 1998.

Olsen, Raymond T. "Managing for Outcomes: Performance Management Strategies Showing Promise," *The Public Manager*, Volume 26, Number 1, 1997.

"Pay and Performance," *Credit Union Magazine*, Volume 63, Number 7, July 1, 1997.

Payne, Tim. "Editorial: 360-Degree Assessment and Feedback," *International Journal of Selection and Assessment*, Volume 6, Number 1, January 1, 1998.

"Performance Management: Encouraging Great Performance," *HR Focus: American Management Association's Human Resources Publication*, January 1998.

"Performance Management: Helping Supervisors Define Standards of Performance," *HR Focus: American Management Association's Human Resources Publication*, February 1998.

Pollack, David M., and Leslie J. Pollack. "Using 360-Degree Feedback in Performance Appraisal," *Public Personnel Management*, Volume 25, Number 4, 1996.

Rosti, Robert T. Jr., and Frank Shipper. "A Study of the Impact of Training in a Management Development Program Based on 360-Degree Feedback," *Journal of Managerial Psychology*, Volume 13, Number 1–2, 1998.

Venardos, Thomas J., and David L. Geary. "Consulting Success Using Higher Performance Standards," *Public Relations Review*, Volume 23, Number 4, 1997.

Waldman, David A., Leanne E. Atwater, and David Antonioni. "Has 360-Degree Feedback Gone Amok?" *The Academy of Management Executive*, Volume 12, Number 2, 1998.

Watson, Scott. "Five Easy Pieces to Performance Management," *Training & Development*, Volume 52, Number 5, 1998.

Wilson, G. Stuart. "Self / Team Control," *Strategies*, July 1, 1998.

"Work / Life: Performance Management Through a Work / Life Lens," *HR Focus: American Management Association's Human Resources Publication*, February 1998.

ADDITIONAL REFERENCES

"360-Degree Vendor Comparison," available at *HR Magazine Online:* *http://nefried.com/360/360goldshootout.html*

Bearley, Ed D., and John E. Jones. *360-Degree Feedback: Strategies, Tactics and Techniques for Developing Leaders,* 1996.

Berlet, Richard K., and Douglas M. Cravens. *Performance Pay As a Competitive Weapon: A Compensation Policy Model for the 1990s.* New York: John Wiley and Sons, Inc., 1991.

"Case Study No. 39 Office of Multicultural Interests, Team-Based Key Performance Indicators," *The Productive Edge* web site: *http://www.sengai.com.au/c39-omi.htm*

Center for Employee Development web site: *http://www.centerpointsystems.com*

CenterPoint Systems Inc. web site: *http://www.centerpointsystems.com*

Cournoyer, Tammy, TSgt. "Performance Feedback Is Important," *Air Force News,* June 1995, and web site: *http://www.af.mil/news/Jun1995/ n19950622_658.html* June 1995.

Davis, Rogers, Assistant Vice Chancellor, Human Resources, UCSD. "Choosing Performance Management: A Holistic Approach," *CUPA Journal,* Summer 1995.

Fried, N. Elizabeth. "Comparing Features with Needs," *HR Magazine,* December 1998.

Guide to Performance Management. University of California, San Diego, Human Resources Department, 1995. Web site: *http://www-hr.ucsd.edu/~ staffeducation/guide*

Hofrichter, David A., Thomas P. Flannery, and Paul E. Platten, The Hay Group staff. *People Performance and Pay: Dynamic Compensation for Changing Organizations.* The Free Press, 1995.

Lancaster, Hal. "Managing Your Career: Performance Reviews Are More Valuable When More Join In," *Wall Street Journal,* July 9, 1996.

Maynard, Michelle. "Evaluations Evolve From Bottom Up: Workers, Peers Rate Managers." *USA TODAY*, August 3, 1994.

Olivio, Tom. "Giving Employees a Stake in the Outcome: Even Small Companies Can Offer Ownership." MSNBC web site: *http://www.msnbc.com/ news/229381.asp* January 14, 1999.

O'Reilly, Brian. "360-Degree Feedback Can Change Your Life," *Fortune*, October 17, 1994.

"Performance Management," The Aubrey Daniels web site: *www.aubreydaniels.com/pm_description.htm*

Seashore, Charles, and Edith Seashore. *What Did You Say?: The Art of Giving and Receiving Feedback*. North Attleborough, MA: Douglas Charles Press, 1992.

"Success Story: Chase Manhattan Bank." The Accumen web site: *http://www.acumen.com/chasem.html*

"The Continuing Search for Performance Excellence." The Conference Board, Inc., 1998.

INDEX

ABOUT THE AUTHOR

Andrew E. Schwartz is president of A.E. Schwartz & Associates, a Boston-based training and consulting organization (*http://www.aeschwartz.com*). Mr. Schwartz offers management and professional development programs with workbooks and practical solutions to organizational problems. He conducts over 150 programs annually and consults nationally for clients in government, industry, Fortune 500 companies, and nonprofit companies. He is often found at conferences as a keynote presenter or facilitator. His style is fast-paced, participatory, practical, succinct, and enjoyable.

Mr. Schwartz's considerable professional experience includes: Founder of *http://www.trainingconsortium.com* (a searchable database to find trainers, consultants, and speakers); former Training Director for the Smaller Business Association of New England; and former Manager of Training at the Massachusetts Institute of Technology (Information Services).

Mr. Schwartz is very involved in the growth and educational aspects of the training industry. He has authored more than 200 articles on management and professional development and such publications as *The School for Managers, Delegating Authority, Making Dynamic Presentations, Creative Problem Solving*, and *Stress Management*, and has developed 14 titles for the American Management Association's *New Business Success Series*, including *Speaking & Listening Skills, Leadership Skills, Negotiating Skills, How to Build Team Skills*, and *Motivation / Goal Setting*.

More selected BARRON'S titles:

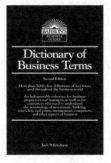
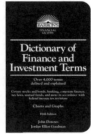